What people are saying about …

HIDDEN PROPHETS OF THE BIBLE

"Michael Williams invites readers to blow the dust off the frequently neglected pages in their Bibles known as the Minor Prophets. Only minor in name, these biblical authors have major truths to teach us about God, His people, and even the gospel. Don't miss out on this life-changing journey of rediscovering these hidden prophets of the Old Testament."

Shaun Tabatt, host of *The Shaun Tabatt Show*

"Michael Williams has done it again. First, he explains the high point of reading Scripture in his *How to Read the Bible through the Jesus Lens*. Now, he probes more deeply into the Minor Prophets with a highly readable book called *Hidden Prophets of the Bible*. One of the least read parts of all Scripture can now be better understood as it points to the coming and future work of Jesus Christ. This new book is a must read."

Charles Morris, president of Haven Ministries

"Often ignored, the Minor Prophets are rich in theological insight and significance for our lives. Michael Williams creatively and masterfully introduces us to the message these men present to their original audiences and show how they anticipate the gospel. I recommend this book for all who want to grow in their knowledge of the Bible."

Tremper Longman III, Robert H. Gundry
Professor of Biblical Studies at Westmont College

"*Hidden Prophets of the Bible* is a practical travel guide through the important terrain of short prophetic books of the Old Testament. With consistent markers for the journey, the reader will find vistas to see, themes to explore, and discussion questions to center additional learning. Professor Michael Williams is an experienced tour guide who provides context, insights, and nuggets of wisdom for lay leaders and pastors alike. More preaching, teaching, and Bible studies from the Minor Prophets are sure to result as people explore these sometimes forgotten, but still highly relevant, biblical texts. After all, the gospel is promised, revealed, and proclaimed there if we take the time to stop, listen, and learn. I encourage you to take the trip and make sure to take this guide!"

Jul Medenblik, president of Calvin
Theological Seminary

HIDDEN PROPHETS
OF THE BIBLE

HIDDEN PROPHETS OF THE BIBLE

FINDING THE GOSPEL IN
HOSEA THROUGH MALACHI

MICHAEL WILLIAMS

David C Cook
transforming lives together

HIDDEN PROPHETS OF THE BIBLE
Published by David C Cook
4050 Lee Vance Drive
Colorado Springs, CO 80918 U.S.A.

David C Cook U.K., Kingsway Communications
Eastbourne, East Sussex BN23 6NT, England

The graphic circle C logo is a registered trademark of David C Cook.

All rights reserved. Except for brief excerpts for review purposes,
no part of this book may be reproduced or used in any form
without written permission from the publisher.

The website addresses recommended throughout this book are offered as a
resource to you. These websites are not intended in any way to be or imply an
endorsement on the part of David C Cook, nor do we vouch for their content.

All Scripture quotations are taken from the Holy Bible, NEW INTERNATIONAL
VERSION®, NIV®. Copyright © 1973, 2011 by Biblica, Inc.® Used by permission.
All rights reserved worldwide. NEW INTERNATIONAL VERSION® and
NIV® are registered trademarks of Biblica, Inc. Use of either trademark for
the offering of goods or services requires the prior written consent of Biblica,
Inc. The author has added italics to Scripture quotations for emphasis.

LCCN 2017931920
ISBN 978-1-4347-1130-4
eISBN 978-1-4347-1189-2

© 2017 Michael Williams PhD

The Team: Tim Peterson, Keith Jones, Amy Konyndyk, Susan Murdock
Cover Design: Nick Lee
Cover Photo: Getty Images
Interior Images: The Metropolitan Museum of Art, New York; and Getty Images

Printed in the United States of America
First Edition 2017

1 2 3 4 5 6 7 8 9 10

042817

CONTENTS

ACKNOWLEDGMENTS

The hidden prophets don't deserve to be so. They have made huge contributions to our understanding of God's grand redemptive plan that finds its focus in Jesus Christ. My efforts to elucidate their individual contributions involves another group of hidden individuals. They are the ones whose supporting efforts have made a project such as this possible. They, too, deserve to have their contributions brought out into the light so that they can be duly acknowledged and thanked.

Among these hidden adjuvants are Verne Kenney, Kyle Duncan, Tim Peterson, and Jack Campbell at David C Cook. I am thankful for their suggestion for this project, their enthusiasm and encouragement for it, and their helpfulness, along with that of the entire Cook team, in seeing it through to completion. I could not have asked for more helpful people. They clearly practice what they publish.

Dan DeVries, who assisted my research into several of these hidden prophets, proved to be extremely helpful before he was called away to other adventures in ministry. His humor and keen intellect will be missed around here, but will certainly contribute to his future success in the church and academy.

I must also note my appreciation for the administration of Calvin Theological Seminary, who graciously granted me flexibility in my teaching schedule so that I would be able to complete this exploration into seldom-visited biblical territory. Their vital support and encouragement in this way is certainly hidden, but highly valued.

Finally, I owe a huge debt of gratitude to my wonderful wife and best friend, Dawn, whose steady love and encouragement continue to amaze me. It is a delight to wake up each day to her energizing companionship. I thank her for her active and helpful engagement with all aspects of this work and for her mysterious but evidently unshakable belief in me. Her quiet support and self-sacrifice are truly a picture of Christlikeness.

INTRODUCTION

At the very end of the Old Testament lies a collection of books that are reminiscent of small towns throughout the country—ones situated along routes no longer frequented once the interstate system was installed. These towns have all sorts of fascinating things to offer the occasional visitor. One can, for example, find educational and awe-inspiring wonders such as Biosphere 2[1] or the largest tree on earth,[2] along with striking exemplars of quirkiness such as the world's largest ball of twine[3] or the International Banana Museum.[4] Sadly, despite their superabundance of captivating curiosities, these small towns can't compete with the traffic and attention drawn by their larger neighbors along the more traveled highways.

Like many of these towns, these small, prophetic books lie almost forgotten in their biblical backwater. They remain tucked away, hidden from view, obscured by the shadows of such giants as Ezekiel and Daniel on one side and the Gospels on the other. It is high time we visited these hidden prophets of the Bible. We need to be reminded of the reason why they have been included in Holy Scripture. In this book we will discover that they, too, offer the occasional visitor unique perspectives and insights couched in quirky and profound details. Like visitors to America's small towns, visitors to these books will leave both delighted and educated.

The fact that these hidden prophets are much shorter than their canonically preceding colleagues has resulted in the application of an unfortunate moniker to these twelve compositions: the "Minor Prophets." Such a designation might suggest to the casual biblical tourist that the content of these books is of "minor" importance. But such is not the case at all! The term *minor* does not refer to their significance; instead, it is solely a description of their length. Though short on word count, each one of these prophets is long on rhetorical power and redemptive relevance. Perhaps surprising to some, what these Minor Prophets reveal to those who stop by to visit is nothing less than the gospel of Jesus Christ!

At this point, I can sense some skepticism among readers of the travel guide. If these prophets contain visit-worthy gospel exhibits, you may ask, how come you've never heard about them before? There are no doubt at least a couple of reasons why these gems remain undiscovered, hidden from the view and appreciation of the larger Christian public. We have already pointed out their unfortunate location in the collection of biblical books we call the canon. Another reason for their neglect may be simply because of the fact that they are, after all, *prophetic* books. Labeling a book "prophetic" is like labeling a neighborhood "in transition." The term suggests something unsettled and perhaps even dangerous. We are all aware of how prophetic literature has been misused throughout history to justify all sorts of social upheaval, political causes, and end-time predictions. Those of us having a more timid disposition might deem it advisable to avoid the neighborhood of the prophets altogether and drive straight on through to the Gospels without stopping. But doing so would be shortchanging ourselves as much as flying to France without learning any French.

The prophets, including the Minor Prophets, help us understand what it is that we are going to be encountering in the Gospels. That is, they enable us to translate the gospel. In fact, the New Testament is quite clear that the prophetic books actually *contain* the gospel. They give us the gospel before we get to the Gospels! Indeed, the apostle Paul begins his letter to the church at Rome by saying that the gospel he proclaims is nothing less than the gospel God "promised beforehand through his prophets in the Holy Scriptures regarding his Son" (Romans 1:2–3).

In this book, therefore, we are going to take some time to consider the gospel that the prophets were talking about. We're going to motor right in, park the car, and look around for a while to make sure that we give ourselves the opportunity to see all the amazing things these books have to offer, things that have been hidden away from us for far too long.

So we'll plan our itinerary through the Minor Prophets to include a leisurely stop at the home of each one of these twelve men. As we investigate the environs of each of these remote and unfamiliar territories, we'll be on the lookout for any details that will inform and enrich our time there, including:

- *Little-known facts about the prophet*
  We'll poke around to uncover curious and interesting details about the prophet's life

and the book he left behind for us to read. These details could include the historical circumstances in which the prophet lived and worked, surviving material or literary artifacts from the prophet's time, parallels between the prophet's circumstances and those of his ancient Near Eastern neighbors, legends and traditions associated with the prophet, and insights that a close analysis of the original language of the prophet's writings might provide for us.

- *The gospel according to the prophet*
  Not only does the apostle Paul tell us that the prophetic writings contain the gospel (Romans 1:2–3), but Jesus himself does! When the resurrected Jesus came and, without being recognized, walked along with a couple of his disciples who were returning home to Emmaus from Jerusalem, the gospel writer Luke tells us that Jesus dispelled their confusion by explaining to them "what was said in all the Scriptures concerning himself ... beginning with Moses *and all the Prophets*" (Luke 24:27). So we'll take some time to explore how each prophet provides his own contribution to our understanding of who Christ is and what he has done.

- *Why the prophet should matter to you*

  Because the gospel message concerns all of us, and because the gospel message is also communicated by each of the prophets, their unique messages have necessary consequences for us now. We'll mull over the connection between the things we find in each prophetic book and the gospel implications of those things that can inform the diverse situations we find ourselves in today.

- *Discussion questions*

  After any stopover at an unfamiliar place, some time to reflect on the adventure is always helpful. We'll conclude our visit to each Minor Prophet with some questions that naturally arise from our contemplation of the experience. These questions will stimulate discussion and reflection as we suggest to ourselves potential contemporary situations and challenges for which the prophetic material provides an essential word. Thinking about these things will help us see how our prophetic road trip has left us more seasoned travelers on the path of life.

This book will therefore uncover what has been blocked from our view, shine light on what has been concealed in the shadows, and recall to our minds what has been forgotten within the writings of this group of little-known prophets coming at the very end of the Old Testament. The wonderful insights, perspectives, guidance, and gospel witness of these prophets will once again be exposed to the light of day. I trust that you will find your visit to these hidden prophets to be well worth the trip.

HOSEA

The first exit off the expressway from the Major Prophets leads directly to the book of Hosea, which lies hidden behind a tangled overgrowth of misunderstanding, fear, and neglect. When we continue past these insubstantial but often effective barriers, we encounter Hosea himself, who launches into his prophecy by describing with unpleasant vividness his dysfunctional relationship with a woman of dubious reputation. Whenever we are confronted with other people's relational dirty laundry, it can make us squirm with discomfort. But after spending some time with him, we discover that Hosea, by means of his woebegone tale, is presenting us with some fundamental truths of the gospel that would only be fully realized over six hundred years later. Wiping away the dust and grime from this window into God's redemptive plan reveals the pure gold hidden inside this book. Let's take some time here to explore this seldom-visited treasure that Hosea has prepared for us.

LITTLE-KNOWN FACTS ABOUT HOSEA

1. Hosea is a mysterious person.

Everything we know about Hosea comes from the first verses of his book—and it isn't very much at all. He is introduced merely as "Hosea son of Beeri" (1:1). The identification of Hosea's father is also a mystery, and we get no help from the meaning of his name. In Hebrew, Beeri means "my well" and may simply refer to a feature of the place where he was born. The only other time the name Beeri occurs in the Bible is Genesis 26:34. But there it is the name of a different, earlier individual: a Hittite, who was one of Esau's fathers-in-law. Outside of the Bible, a surviving tradition maintains Beeri was also a prophet and that two verses of his prophecy were later inserted into the book of Isaiah (8:19–20).[1] Also, tradition holds that Beeri died in the exile.[2]

We also do not know the city in which Hosea lived. Nor do we know how old he was when he started his ministry. We cannot even pinpoint precisely the period during which Hosea prophesied. In the opening verse, we're told that he prophesied during the reigns of four kings of the southern kingdom of Judah, a period that overlapped the reign of Jeroboam II in the northern kingdom of Israel. But the reign of the first southern king mentioned (Uzziah) began in 792 BC, and the reign of the last southern king mentioned (Hezekiah) ended in 686 BC. That's a period of over one hundred years![3] The mysterious prophet Hosea was active *sometime* during this tumultuous period in history that would see the collapse of the northern kingdom of Israel in 722 BC at the hands of the Assyrian war machine led by Shalmaneser V and his successor, Sargon II.

Further, we cannot even be certain that Hosea wrote the book that bears his name. Some other individual or group of individuals may have written at least parts of the book. The opening verses all refer to Hosea in the third person: "The word of the LORD that came to Hosea" (1:1; note, not "to *me*"); "When the LORD began to speak through Hosea" (1:2; note, not "through *me*"); and "Then the LORD said to Hosea" (1:4, 6; note, not "to *me*"). It would be strange for Hosea to refer to himself in the third person. However, chapter 3 does include a few first-person references: "The LORD said to me" (3:1); "So I bought her" (3:2); "Then I told her, 'You are to live with me ... and I will behave the same way'" (3:3).

We are provided with tantalizingly brief snippets of information concerning Hosea's life in an extrabiblical composition entitled *Lives of the Prophets*. This document is dated as early as c. AD 1 and claims to inform readers of "the names of the prophets, and where they are from, and where they died and how, and where they lie."[4] Concerning Hosea, we're told:

> This man was from Belemoth of the tribe of Issachar, and he was buried in his own district in peace. And he gave a portent, that the LORD would arrive upon the earth if ever the oak which is in Shiloh were divided from itself, and twelve oaks came to be. (5:1–2)[5]

Although we would love answers to the many questions raised by these sentences, those answers remain as hidden and mysterious as the prophet Hosea himself.

Sadly, we do not know with certainty when or how the prophet died. We are also not entirely sure where he was buried, although a Jewish tradition offers further details surrounding this event. The tradition maintains that Hosea requested before his death in Babylon that his remains be loaded onto a camel that would then be allowed to choose its own course back to the Promised Land. Wherever the camel stopped was where Hosea should be buried. His instructions were followed, and the camel eventually completed its journey, stopping, so the tradition goes, in the Jewish cemetery of Safed—a town in the northern district of modern Israel. And so it is believed by many today that this is Hosea's final resting place.[6]

2. Hosea is the only writing prophet to come from Israel.

Of the sixteen biblical prophets who have books named after them in the Bible, Hosea is the only one who actually lived in the northern kingdom of Israel. So Hosea is prophesying to a nation in which he himself is a resident. Other writing prophets prophesied to the northern kingdom of Israel, but Hosea is the only one who actually made his home among them. How do we know this when the location of his birth and ministry are not explicitly mentioned? Hosea writes in a difficult Hebrew that is identified with that of the northern kingdom of Israel. Also, he repeatedly mentions the Israelite cities of Jezreel (1:4, 5, 11; 2:22), Gibeah (5:8; 9:9; 10:9), Bethel (10:15; 12:4), and Samaria—the capital of the northern kingdom (7:1; 8:5, 6; 10:5, 7; 13:16). Moreover, Hosea uses the name Ephraim in addressing his audience—thirty-seven times! At the time of Hosea's composition, this name is used exclusively to refer to the northern kingdom.

3. God commands Hosea to marry a promiscuous woman.

The precise meaning of what God is commanding Hosea to do, however, is hotly debated. Is God commanding Hosea to marry a woman who is already sexually active? Does Gomer only become unfaithful after she marries Hosea? Key to understanding what is intended is the Hebrew word translated as "promiscuous": *zenûnîm*. This word has the general meaning of "inclined to fornicate."[7] To fornicate is to have consensual sex with someone with whom you are not married. A woman who, like Gomer, is described as inclined toward sex with men outside of marriage we might describe today as "loose." Her relaxed sexual standards toward multiple partners appear to have nothing to do with whether she is in a marriage relationship. So God is commanding Hosea to marry a woman who is already sexually promiscuous and who will prove to continue to be sexually promiscuous even after he marries her. Poor Hosea!

But would God really command Hosea to marry such a woman? Some point to Leviticus 21:7 and 14, for example, as an indication that such a command would be inconsistent with God's expressed will.[8] But the biblical prohibitions against such a marriage pertain to priests, and there is nothing that suggests Hosea was a priest.

If it was against God's law for Hosea to marry a woman who was characteristically unfaithful, then it would be against God's law for

God himself to enter into any relationship with any human being—ever—for we are also characteristically unfaithful! The union of a faithful, long-suffering relationship partner with one who is relentlessly unfaithful is, after all, the main point of Hosea's acted-out prophecy.

4. Hosea is a literary artist.

Hosea utilizes almost every implement in his prophetic toolbox to describe Israel's rebellion against God, her unfaithfulness to him, and her dismal spiritual condition. Hosea employs this literary artistry to conjure up in our minds unforgettable images. With a dazzling array of similes and metaphors, Hosea depicts Israel as fundamentally flawed people, plants, animals, and things:

Flawed people
- a cheating wife (3:1–2)
- a person with sores and sickness (5:13)
- a fair-weather friend (6:4)
- a farmer who sows wind and gets a whirlwind for his troubles (8:7)
- a headstrong, ungrateful child (11:1–4)
- a baby without enough sense to come out of the womb (13:13)

Flawed plants
- a blighted, withered, fruitless plant (9:16)
- a vine spreading poison (10:1)

Flawed animals
- a stubborn heifer (4:16)
- a dove fluttering aimlessly (7:11)
- an untamable, wild donkey (8:9)
- a heifer grown accustomed to easy work (10:11–13)

Flawed things
- an oven whose thermostat is stuck on high (7:4–7)
- a half-baked loaf (7:8)
- a faulty bow (7:16)
- something no one has any use for (8:8)
- ephemeral morning mist, vanishing early dew, dissipating chaff and smoke (13:3)

But Hosea also holds out hope for this seemingly hopeless nation. After the judgment their unfaithfulness has brought upon them, God will surprisingly again be merciful to them and bless them. And once again, Hosea uses word pictures to describe God's people at this future time. As a consequence of God's unmerited, unlimited, and generative love, they will be like

- birds who respond to his call (11:11) when they flutter back to him; and
- a blossoming lily, a cedar of Lebanon, a beautiful olive tree, flourishing grain, and a blossoming vine (14:5–7), enjoying God's abundant life and protection.

Hosea's kaleidoscopic, picturesque characterizations are not limited to Israel; he uses similes and metaphors to describe the Lord as well. The Lord coming in judgment Hosea depicts as

- a moth or rot (5:12) that will slowly but inevitably consume the nation;
- a lion, a leopard, or a bear that will tear them to pieces and carry them off (5:14; 13:7–8); and
- one who catches birds with a net (7:12).

But when the Lord comes with mercy and blessing, Hosea pictures him as

- a husband wooing a wife (2:14–16);
- a loving parent who lifts a child to their cheek and teaches them how to walk (11:3–4); and
- a flourishing juniper, enabling the fruitfulness of Israel (14:8).

Even the individual words Hosea uses to paint these word pictures are artfully selected.[9] He uses, for example, words that are found nowhere else in the Bible. The uniqueness of these words gives headaches to translators of English versions, who must search context and related languages for best guesses at their meaning. These include the words translated as "unfaithfulness" (*na'fûfîm*, 2:2), "gifts" (*habhābay*, 8:13), "spreading" (*bôqēq*, 10:1), "evildoers" (*'alwāh*, 10:9), and "burning heat" (*tal'ubôt*, 13:5).

Another literary strategy Hosea uses to force the reader or listener to slow down and give closer attention to his words is the utilization of assonance and alliteration. These literary devices use words that contain and/or begin with similar-sounding letters that could cause tongue twisting if not pronounced carefully. Consider an example from English: "The sixth sick sheik's sixth sheep's sick."[10] The close proximity and sound of the *s*, *sh*, and *th* sounds guarantee that no one is going to be able to say this sentence quickly. This literary feature also adds to the beauty of the composition. It is pleasing to the mind and ear. These carefully constructed expressions are usually impossible to carry over from one language to another, so they are often not visible in English translations. But if we render the Hebrew letters into English ones, this literary device becomes clearer. One example is found in Hosea 4:16, where the words "stubborn" (occurring twice) and "Israel" share, in Hebrew, the *s* and *r* sounds, as seen when we render them in English letters: *sōrērāh sārar yiśrā'ēl*. What a clever way to cause the *form* of the prophecy to emphasize its content! The point Hosea is making, that "Israel is stubborn," has a lot more force when it has to be heard or read slowly.

We cannot leave a consideration of Hosea's writing skill without a brief consideration of how he frequently uses wordplays to make his prophecy unforgettable. Unfortunately, these almost never make their way from Hebrew to English, so their presence in the book of Hosea usually remains hidden. But in the original language, these plays on words have striking effect. One example is the way Hosea plays on the letters of the name Ephraim (which stands for Israel) to show how they correspond to the nation's situation. In Hebrew, the consonants of Israel's other name, Ephraim, are *'-p-r-y-m*. Hosea often repurposes these consonants to link his prophecy to this rebellious nation literarily. So, for example, *'-p-r-y-m* is likened, both in their character and in their spelling, to a stubborn heifer (*p-r-h*, 4:16), a wild donkey (*p-r- '*, 8:9), a worthless plant that produces no fruit (*p-r-y*, 9:16), and a nation unaware that God is the One who heals them (*r-p- '-t-y-m*, 11:3).

Discovering all of this hidden literary artistry in the words of this hidden prophet is like finding a Rembrandt in the back room of a general store in Smalltown, USA. Almost no one knew it existed, much less that it would be found *there*. It makes us wonder what else we might have been missing and need to discover during our visit with Hosea.

5. The meaning of names is hugely significant in Hosea's prophecy.

The names of the principal characters in this prophetic drama also contribute to the force of Hosea's message.

The meaning of the name of Hosea's wife, Gomer, comes from a root meaning "to bring to an end, complete."[11] How appropriate that the unfaithful wife, the one who symbolizes unfaithful Israel, should have a name that points toward the judgment that their unfaithfulness will bring about. God says he "will put an end to the kingdom of Israel" (1:4).

The judgment that will come upon the unfaithful relationship partner is also indicated by the names of Hosea's three children by Gomer. The first son is named Jezreel, meaning "God scatters."

God will scatter the tribes of the northern kingdom among the nations as a consequence of their unfaithfulness.

The name of the second child, a daughter, is Lo-Ruhamah, which means "not loved." The aspect of judgment represented by this name is explained by God himself: "I will no longer show love to Israel, that I should at all forgive them" (1:6).

The third and last of these prophetically significant children is named Lo-Ammi, which means "not my people." This last name is devastatingly powerful in its implications. In the ancient Near East, a man could bring about the legal dissolution of a marriage by simply proclaiming before witnesses, "You are not my wife, and I am not your husband."[12] Therefore, when God says, "You are not my people [*lō' ammî*], and I am not your God" (1:9), he is, in effect, initiating a divorce. For a nation whose identity exclusively resides in its unique, covenantal relationship with God, the dissolution of that relationship is a blow to the very heart of what it means to be Israel!

In stark contrast to the significance of the names of Hosea's wife and children is the significance of Hosea's own name. The contrast is just as profound as the contrast in relational faithfulness between God and his people. Gomer, Jezreel, Lo-Ruhamah, and Lo-Ammi are all names pointing toward the coming judgment for unfaithfulness. But the name Hosea means "He [Yahweh] delivered" or "Deliver!" Either possible translation reminds the unfaithful party of the place—the only place—where deliverance from their well-deserved judgment can be found. Yahweh has brought about deliverance in the past, and it is from him alone that any possible deliverance will come in the future.

6. The book of Hosea is the first, but not the longest, book of the Minor Prophets.

Although the book of Hosea leads in canonical order, it is not the longest book of the Minor Prophets. That distinction is held by the book of Zechariah, whose prophecy contains 2,740 words (in Hebrew), while Hosea checks in at a distant second with 1,996 words (in Hebrew). The book of Hosea comes first among the Minor Prophets not because of its length, therefore, but because it was thought to be the first in *chronological* order.

7. How the people received or responded to Hosea and his prophecy is never recorded.

Almost all of Hosea's book consists of the words of his prophetic messages. The only narrative passages (1:1–2:1 and 3:1–5, only seventeen verses) involve instructions or descriptions of Hosea's interactions with his wife and the symbolic significance of those interactions. Readers are never told how the populace responded to Hosea. Did they ignore him? Did they conclude he was a fringe, irrelevant religious figure? Did they conspire to silence him? Did at least a segment of society take his prophecy to heart and repent? No one knows. But at least *we're* interested in what he has to say! And no doubt *our* response will be appropriate.

8. Hosea has his own holiday!

Hosea is remembered with a feast day (October 17 on the Julian calendar and October 30 on the modern Gregorian calendar) on the liturgical calendar of the Greek Orthodox Church.[13]

In the book of the anniversaries of the martyrs and other saints commemorated by the Roman Catholic Church, the prophet Hosea (Osee) is remembered on the fourth of July.[14] So the next time you throw some burgers on the grill as part of your celebration of US independence, remember Hosea!

THE GOSPEL ACCORDING TO HOSEA

So what, if anything, do the words of an Israelite wordsmith who is stuck in a relationship with a congenitally unfaithful woman have to do with the gospel of Jesus Christ? The word *gospel* means "good news," and there seems to be precious little of that in this book for Hosea! His wife, Gomer, is described as "promiscuous," "adulterous," and "unfaithful." She holds her morality as loosely as a new parent holds a dirty diaper—regarding it as an unwelcome part of life, to be held at arm's length (when necessary to be held at all) and jettisoned at the earliest possible opportunity.

God uses the sad circumstances that make up the soap opera of Hosea's marriage to draw a parallel between Gomer's infidelity and that of his people. Like an unfaithful wife, they, too, "have deserted the LORD" (4:10), "a spirit of prostitution is in their heart," and "they do not acknowledge the LORD" (5:4). If we are at all objective, we have to conclude that Gomer certainly does not deserve the love that Hosea keeps lavishing on her. And Israel doesn't deserve the love God keeps lavishing on them. Of course, when we arrive at this negative judgment of Gomer and Israel, we also arrive at a negative judgment of ourselves, because we are no different.

Hosea had committed himself to a marriage relationship with a partner who habitually failed to honor it. And God had committed himself to a relationship with a people who habitually failed to honor it. In fact, throughout history, human beings have never honored any relationship we have entered into with God. For any relationship to exist and flourish, there must be commitment and faithfulness on the part of both partners. But the human side of any potential divine-human relationship contains a genetic defect in this regard. We are just as incapable of faithfulness to God as Gomer was incapable of faithfulness to Hosea. The apostle Paul lays it all on the table:

> There is no one righteous, not even one;
>> there is no one who understands;
>> there is no one who seeks God.
> All have turned away,
>> they have together become worthless;
> there is no one who does good,
>> not even one. (Romans 3:10–12)

Clearly, there is no hope possible from our end for a different future outcome for any relationship we enter into with God. Any hope at all, as unlikely and as unmerited as it is, would have to come from God himself.

Surprisingly, through Hosea, God promises just such a different future! With amazing grace, God declares to his people that he "will heal their waywardness and love them freely" (14:4). He won't abandon them to experience the pain, brokenness, and ruin that inevitably result from their rejection of him. Instead, he "will deliver this people from the power of the grave" and "will redeem them from death" (13:14). Now that is good news! But how on earth could that even be possible when dealing with relationship partners whose morals are looser than a shar-pei's skin? The answer, of course, is that it isn't possible on earth. The answer comes from heaven.

The only possible way for there to be a lasting, secure, unbreakable relationship between the perfectly faithful God and fundamentally flawed human beings is for human beings to become perfectly faithful as well. And that is precisely why God became a human being—to accomplish on our behalf what we are incapable of accomplishing ourselves. He upholds the human side of the divine-human relationship by providing a perfect human being, God himself in the flesh, to be our representative. For all of us who by faith claim Jesus as our perfect human representative, our relationship with God is now just as uninterrupted as Jesus's faithfulness on our behalf.

In other words, by faith, Jesus's righteousness is counted as our righteousness. That spiritual wardrobe change is what is being described in Revelation 19:7–8 as the characteristic clothing of the faithful bride of Christ: "Fine linen, bright and clean, was given her to wear." Notice that the fine linen was *given* to her. It is not something she earned or otherwise obtained through her own efforts. The passage goes on to say that "fine linen stands for the righteous acts of God's holy people," but this is gospel shorthand. We are told elsewhere that "all our righteous acts are like filthy rags" (Isaiah 64:6)—hardly the equivalent of "fine linen"! What the verse in Revelation means is that Jesus's righteous acts are *given* to his people and credited as their own righteous acts. It is this "fine linen" alone that provides us access to the wedding supper of the Lamb (Matthew 22:1–14). It is the faithfulness of Jesus that makes the church a faithful bride.

The New Testament alludes to the prophecy of Hosea when it reflects on the benefits of Jesus's faithfulness on our behalf. Because Jesus secures for us an unbreakable, everlasting relationship with God, the significance of the names of Hosea's children no longer applies. In fact, just the opposite is true. The name of Hosea's first child was Jezreel, meaning "God scatters." But through faith in Jesus Christ, God is now *gathering* people "from every tribe and language and people and nation" (Revelation 5:9). The name of Hosea's second child was Lo-Ruhamah, meaning "not loved." But Jesus reverses this meaning as well, because "God demonstrates his own love for us in this: While we were still sinners, Christ died for us" (Romans 5:8). And the name of Hosea's third child was Lo-Ammi, meaning "not my people." This dissolution of the relationship is reversed through the faithfulness of Jesus Christ on our behalf, so that now those who trust in him "are the people of God" (1 Peter 2:10).

The gospel according to Hosea is the good news of a loving God who is so inexplicably and yet relentlessly committed to loving his people that he will do whatever it takes to secure his relationship with them. In the New Testament, we learn that God's relentless love and desire for a relationship with us even extends to the sacrifice of his own Son. The choice for every human being is clear: either a miserable existence where "there is no faithfulness, no love, no acknowledgement of God in the land," where "there is only cursing, lying and murder, stealing and adultery," where "they break all bounds, and bloodshed follows bloodshed" (that sounds like the evening news), and where, consequently, "the land dries up, and all who live in it waste away" (Hosea 4:1–3) or a rich, abundant life in relationship with God through Jesus Christ, where his people "will flourish like the grain," "blossom like the vine," and their fame "will be like the wine of Lebanon" (Hosea 14:7). The good news is that we don't have to be Gomers anymore!

WHY HOSEA SHOULD MATTER TO YOU

There is a nagging uncertainty that frequently besets new believers and also believers who have spent a significant amount of time wandering at the outer edges of faith. Seasoned believers aren't immune from it either. Those so afflicted wrestle with an assurance of their salvation. They realize all too well how far short they fall from the spiritual ideal. They hardly need hellfire and brimstone sermons to convince them of their shortcomings. They are quite aware of those, thank you very much! And if the church pews are to be populated only by the saintly, or those who pretend to be so, then those who are painfully aware of their deficiencies feel unwelcome and understandably question their legitimate inclusion among such a group. They conclude that maybe they aren't "saved" after all.

The book of Hosea should matter to us because it directly addresses the basis for confidence in our relationship with God. And that confidence has nothing to do with the worthiness of any of us. The message of Hosea is that we are all as worthy of God's love as Hosea's immoral wife, Gomer, was worthy of his. That is, we are not worthy of it at all. So if we're looking for something good within us as the basis for God's love for us, then we'll be as successful as someone looking for water in the Sahara. You might think you see it there occasionally, but it always turns out to be just a mirage. No one—not the "saint" in the pew or the "sinner" in the alley—*deserves* God's love. Anyone looking at their own praiseworthiness as the basis for a relationship with God is right to wrestle with the assurance of their salvation, because that assurance cannot be found there.

The prophet Hosea reminds us that it is God himself who is the basis for our confidence in our relationship with him. He is the One who establishes that relationship, even if we can never understand the selfless love and relentless grace that would motivate him to do so. And God himself secures that relationship with him forever by providing the God-man for all of us Gomers. God came in the flesh as Jesus Christ, the *only* perfect human being, to secure an eternal, unbreakable relationship with God for every Gomer who puts faith in him. The fact that our relationship with God is based on his own perfection and not on our imperfection should give us tremendous confidence. We are justified in doubting our relationship with God only if we could imagine God being dissatisfied with the life and sacrifice of Jesus Christ, our representative.

God's love is a forgiving love, and it is a restoring love, but it is also a penetrating love. God's love does not just restore his broken relationship with human beings. It certainly does that. But it also penetrates into those human beings to alter their spiritual genetic structure from the inside out. In other words, God's love makes us new creations (2 Corinthians 5:17) who love him back. Hosea prophesies about a day in the future, a day realized through Christ. God promises his people that, on that day,

> I will betroth you to me forever;
> > I will betroth you in righteousness and
> > > justice,
> > in love and compassion.
> I will betroth you in faithfulness,
> > and you will acknowledge the LORD.
> > > (Hosea 2:19–20)

The five attributes listed—righteousness, justice, love, compassion, and faithfulness—are those that God himself provides on our behalf through Jesus Christ. And they are also those attributes that God causes to be increasingly characteristic of the lives of those in relationship with him. This is the process of sanctification, the work of the Holy Spirit, who enables us to realize more fully the depths of this relationship that has already been secured for us forever. This is the meaning of the Hebrew word (*yd'*) translated as "acknowledge" above. It doesn't mean simple familiarity or assent. In this context, it means an intimate, personal knowledge of the sort shared by married couples whose long, caring, shared experience together has forged them into an inseparable unity. That is the relationship God desires with us. That is the relationship that yields the fullest possible human existence. That is the message of Hosea, and it should matter to every Christian, and indeed to every human being, who searches for meaning, purpose, significance, and security in life.

DISCUSSION QUESTIONS

1. Put yourself in Hosea's shoes. His wife, Gomer, has never reciprocated his love for her. How would you respond to a spouse who treated you like Gomer treated Hosea? Are you treating God that way?

2. Whom do you trust more to be a faithful relationship partner with God: yourself or Jesus? This is not a trick question! You probably know how you're *supposed* to answer, but what is the *real* answer in your everyday life? If it were at all possible for you to be consistently faithful to God, then why would Jesus have come?

3. If the necessary faithfulness in our relationship with God is accomplished by Jesus, then what responsibility, if any, do *we* have in the relationship now? Does what *we* do in our relationship with God have anything to do with what Jesus does *for* us in that relationship?

4. What are some practical ways to evaluate whether and how you are growing in your relationship with God? Is growth in that relationship important to you? Is growth in your relationship with God inevitable because it is the work of the Spirit? How might other believers help you with that growth? How might you help other believers grow in their relationship with God?

5. How would you explain the message of the book of Hosea to someone else? What could or should motivate you to do so? What would you say to someone who doesn't feel good enough to be a Christian?

JOEL

The next stop on our road trip through the Minor Prophets is the much smaller book of the prophet Joel. Although this prophet's name might be recognized because five verses of his prophecy appear at a critical point in the New Testament book of Acts, one would be hard pressed to provide any other information about him. Evidently, there is much about this prophet that remains hidden from plain sight. Even when we pull over and take the time to stroll through the chapters and verses of this tiny book, there are still major barriers to our understanding its message. Chief among these are the details, images, and implications of "the day of the LORD." Joel is the first Minor Prophet to use this term. Understanding what he means by it will be the key to unlocking the hidden message he holds for those who stop by to visit him. But before we start digging in his yard, let's spend some time trying to get to know Joel himself.

LITTLE-KNOWN FACTS ABOUT JOEL

1. Facts about Joel are little known.

Joel is a bit stingy with his personal information. The only biographical information Joel provides us in his prophecy comes at the very beginning—he is the son of a man named Pethuel. Unfortunately, Pethuel is not found anywhere else in Scripture. The name Pethuel most likely means "young man of God"[1] and may at least suggest that Joel came from a God-fearing family.

One Jewish tradition equates the name Pethuel with the name of the judge-prophet Samuel.[2] Adding to the confusion is the fact that Samuel did indeed have a son named Joel (1 Samuel 8:2), who was his firstborn son. But equating this son of Samuel with the prophet Joel presents problems because we're told in 1 Samuel 8:3 that Samuel's sons "did not follow his ways. They turned aside after dishonest gain and accepted bribes and perverted justice." This is hardly acceptable behavior for a biblical prophet! But the tradition wriggles out from under this burden by maintaining that Samuel's sons repented and that it was Abijah who was the really problematic son; Joel's sin was merely that he didn't rein in his brother's evil behavior.[3]

Though this is a fascinating tradition, it is highly unlikely that the prophet Joel is Samuel's son. In fact, there are more than twelve other people named Joel in the Old Testament, and the prophet Joel cannot be identified with any of them either. Samuel anointed Saul to be king in 1050 BC, and we know from Scripture that Samuel's sons were already fully grown at that time. Although, as we'll see shortly, while no one is sure exactly when Joel prophesied, everyone is sure that it was after the eleventh century BC.

2. Among all the Minor Prophets, the date of the book of Joel is the hardest to determine.

Neither the introduction to the book (Joel 1:1) nor the book itself contains any historical data, such as the reign of a king, that would enable a person to confidently date Joel's prophecy. Of course, that has not kept people from trying. Guesses range from as early as the ninth century BC to as late as the second century BC.[4] That's a seven-hundred-year range! Some try to narrow that range a bit by focusing on one piece of evidence available in the book. It seems clear from Joel's prophecy that the temple is in existence. In 1:9, for example, reference is made to grain offerings and drink offerings in the house of the LORD and to the priests who minister there. But whether the first temple (in existence from about 980 BC to 586 BC) or the second temple (completed in 516 BC and destroyed in AD 70) is in view is impossible to say. So we're left with several possible centuries in which Joel could have prophesied!

3. The book of Joel is infested with locusts.

Joel spends about half of his short prophecy focusing on a plague of locusts—its effect on the land and how the people should respond to it. And in 1:4, he uses four different words to describe these locusts: גָּזָם (*gāzām*), אַרְבֶּה (*'arbeh*), יֶלֶק (*yeleq*), and חָסִיל (*ḥāsîl*). The meaning of these words presents a problem for those who want to know precisely what Joel is talking about. Is he describing four different kinds of locusts? Or is he describing four different stages in the life cycle of a locust (larval, partially developed, fully developed, sexually mature)? Or is Joel simply using terms that describe what locusts do ("cut off" vegetation, "devastate" crops, "become numerous," strip foliage, and "consume" everything in their path)? The jury is still out on this question.[5] No matter how these four words are understood, the effect communicated by them is clear.

They signal almost unimaginable damage and destruction. These horrific consequences are described by writer Rachel Nuwer in her coverage of a plague of locusts that descended on Israel as recently as 2013:

> A swarm of locusts will consume any green vegetation in its path—even toxic plants—and can decimate a farmer's field almost as soon as it descends. In one day, the mass of insects can munch its way through the equivalent amount of food as 15 million people consume in the same time period, with billions of insects covering an area up to the size of Cairo, Africa's largest city. As such, at their worst locust swarms can impact some 20 percent of the planet's human population through both direct and indirect damages they cause.[6]

Because of this feared devastation, locusts have been used metaphorically in writings both in the Bible and from the broader ancient

Near East to depict the threat posed by an invading army that could swarm over a country, leaving only desolation and ruin behind it. Just two verses after Joel describes the locusts, he does indeed compare them to an invading army: "A nation has invaded my land, a mighty army without number" (1:6).

Just as locusts can be compared to armies, so armies can be compared to locusts. Consider, for example, how Ramses II of Egypt describes his enemy Muwatallis II of Hatti and all the foreign countries allied to him in the great battle of Qadesh:

> Their rulers were there with him, each man with
> his forces;
> their chariotry was vast in extent, unequalled;
> they covered hill and valley, they were like the
> locust-swarm in their multitude.[7]

Joel uses this fearsome locust imagery from his ancient Near Eastern world to drive home the terrifying reality of the coming "day of the LORD" that "will come like destruction from the Almighty" (1:15).

4. Some verses in Joel's prophecy are similar to an Assyrian prayer.

Parts of an Assyrian prayer contained within a hymn to the goddess Nanaya (Reverse II.24'–28') remind us of Joel's description of the locusts and the devastation they cause.[8]

ṣennu erebu muḫalliq ašna[n]	The evil locust which destroys the crops/grain,
lemnu zirziru mubbil ṣippāti	the wicked dwarf-locust which dries up the orchards,
pārisu sattukkī ša ilī u ištarā[ti]	which cuts off the regular offerings of the gods and goddesses—
šēmēki ᵈEllil *māharki* ᵈTutu	(Verily) Ellil listens to you, and Tutu is before you—
ina qibītiki limmani zaqīqīš	may by your command it be turned into nothing.

The two types of locusts referenced in this prayer—the *erebu* and the *zirziru*—"seem to be distinct species and not different stages in the metamorphosis of a single type of locust."[9] If this is indeed the case, then this perhaps suggests that the four words Joel uses to describe the locusts also signify distinct species.

Also, in the Assyrian prayer above, the devastation wrought by these locusts "cuts off the regular offerings of the gods and goddesses." This description parallels what Joel describes in 1:9, where, because of the locusts, "grain offerings and drink offerings are cut off from the house of the LORD."

What are we to make of this potential parallel? We have to allow that it may be nothing more than coincidence, but one scholar suggests that it is a further indication of Joel's "penchant for traditional rhetoric"—even when that traditional language is drawn from sources beyond Israel's borders![10] Of course, if Joel is, in fact, using extrabiblical sources to make his point, it does not mean that he is endorsing the worldview of the culture that produced those sources. In a similar way, preachers who use sermon illustrations that come from Hollywood movies are not endorsing the worldview of the Hollywood culture that produced those illustrations.

5. Part of Joel's prophecy seems to contradict Isaiah 2:4 and Micah 4:3.

The often-quoted verse of Isaiah 2:4 (repeated in Micah 4:3) is the archetypical expression of the hope for peace: "They will beat their swords into plowshares and their spears into pruning hooks. Nation will not take up sword against nation, nor will they train for war anymore." This inspirational verse is represented on the "Isaiah Wall" in Ralph Bunche Park, across the street from the United Nations building. Allusion to this verse is also made by a bronze sculpture that stands on the North Garden of the United Nations Headquarters. Presented by the former Soviet Union in 1959, it is entitled "Let Us Beat Swords into Plowshares."

Who wouldn't welcome a prophecy such as this, one that assures us of better days ahead when God will break the weapons of war and usher in an age of peace? How jarring it is, then, for us to hear the prophet Joel call out to the nations:

> Prepare for war!
> Rouse the warriors!
>> Let all the fighting men draw near
>> and attack.
> Beat your plowshares into swords
>> and your pruning hooks into spears.
>> (Joel 3:9–10)

Wait just a minute! Is this a contradiction in Scripture? Should we beat our swords into plowshares or our plowshares into swords? How are we supposed to understand what Joel is saying here? The answer to this question reveals the danger of taking isolated passages of Scripture out of the larger contexts that give them meaning. Joel is talking about the same thing as Isaiah and Micah—but from a different perspective. Isaiah and Micah speak of a time of blessing that will come after a time of judgment. Joel speaks of a time of coming judgment that has to occur before a time of blessing can be realized. Joel calls this pivotal perspective from which both the coming judgment and coming blessing must be viewed the "day of the LORD." We'll explore this pivotal concept later in the chapter.

6. Joel has his own holiday too!

On the calendar of feasts and fasts for the Greek Orthodox Church, Joel's feast day is October 19 (on the Julian calendar, corresponding to November 1 on the modern Gregorian calendar).[11]

In the book of the anniversaries of the martyrs and other saints commemorated by the Roman Catholic Church, the prophet Joel is remembered on July 13.[12]

7. There are at least four competing traditions regarding Joel's death and burial.

According to one tradition, Joel is buried not far from the prophet Hosea. Hosea is believed to be buried in the Jewish cemetery in the town of Safed.[13] Located a mere five miles northwest of Safed is the

Arab village of al-Jish (in Hebrew, Gush Ḥalav), situated on the ruins of a once prosperous city. There, this tradition maintains, the prophet Joel is buried.[14]

However, a Roman Catholic tradition preserved by the Benedictine monks of St. Augustine's Abbey notes that the location of Joel's body "is said to be enshrined under the high altar of the cathedral of Zara in Dalmatia."[15]

A very early tradition preserved in *Lives of the Prophets* (8:1–2) tells us that Joel died in peace in the territory of Reuben, where he was from.[16]

Unfortunately, a less peaceful account of Joel's end is preserved in *The Book of the Bee*, a Nestorian Christian sacred history usually dated to the thirteenth century AD. In chapter 32 of this collection of traditions—entitled "Of the Death of the Prophets; How They Died, and (Where) Each One of Them Was Buried"—we learn that "others say that Ahaziah the son of Amaziah smote him with a staff upon his head; and while his life was yet in him, they brought him to his own land, and after two days he died."[17]

THE GOSPEL ACCORDING TO JOEL

So what does a locust plague and "the coming of the great and dreadful day of the LORD" (Joel 2:31) have to do with the gospel of Jesus Christ? More than might be apparent at first glance. One could even say there is a hidden gospel in this hidden prophet!

Joel uses the occasion of the locust plague and all the devastation accompanying it to focus his people's attention on something even worse that is coming in the future—the day of the Lord. The locusts had come as God's punishment for unfaithfulness. Only by turning to the Lord with wholehearted repentance and faith would there be any hope of deliverance (2:12–13). To an even greater degree, in the coming day of the Lord, the judgment of God would come to all nations (3:2). Their faithless rebellion against God is pictured as coming to a climax when they beat their plowshares into swords to fight against him in a place called the Valley of Jehoshaphat (3:2), which means "the Valley where the Lord judges." The Lord will decree the fate of multitudes in that valley of decision (3:14). And his exercise of divine judgment at that time will be absolutely terrifying:

> The sun and moon will be darkened,
> and the stars no longer shine.
> The LORD will roar from Zion
> and thunder from Jerusalem;
> the earth and the heavens will tremble.
> (3:15–16)[18]

In the face of such a cosmic outbreak of almighty wrath, one would think that escape would be impossible. But Joel does indeed hold out to us good news, or gospel. Somehow, he tells us, that day will also include an outpouring of the Spirit and salvation for those who trust in the Lord (2:28–32). God's blessings will be so abundant and rich that they are described as mountains dripping with wine, hills flowing with milk, and ravines gushing with water (3:18).

But if the deciding factor between bad news and good news is our faithfulness to the Lord, then we're all doomed. Not one of us is consistently faithful. If only there were at least one of us who was consistently faithful, one whom we could hold out as our representative. This is the heart of the good news! God has provided just such a person for us in Jesus Christ. He is the only perfect human being who experiences both sides of the day of the Lord for everyone who by faith claims him as their representative. He takes our judgment upon himself and applies his own faithfulness to us.

At the Last Supper, Jesus explained to his disciples that he had come to pay the terrible price for our unfaithfulness, and so remove the barrier to our experience of life in relationship with God. He said, "This cup is the new covenant in my blood, which is poured out for you" (Luke 22:20). In other words, Jesus was saying that the cup of God's wrath against our unfaithfulness that he was about to experience on our behalf would make possible a new relationship with God. But it would come at the cost of his blood. And, indeed, when Jesus paid that price on the cross, the signs in heaven and earth that Joel foretold were realized:

> From noon until three in the afternoon darkness
> came over all the land....
> The earth shook, the rocks split and the tombs
> broke open. (Matthew 27:45, 51–52)

And after Jesus paid the price for our unfaithfulness, the way was clear for our new relationship with God, secured forever by Jesus's faithfulness. So, on the day of Pentecost, the apostle Peter quoted Joel's prophecy to explain the coming of the Holy Spirit and the salvation now freely available to all who by faith claim Jesus as their representative (Acts 2:16–21).

Jesus has experienced the negative aspects of the day of the Lord so that those who trust in him can experience its positive aspects. However, those who reject Jesus will have to face the full negative impact of that coming day on their own. And no one can withstand it (Joel 2:11). Those who instead choose life by turning to God through faith in his Son have nothing to fear on that day. That life is just as extreme as its opposite. And that is the gospel of Joel.

WHY JOEL SHOULD MATTER TO YOU

The book of Joel reminds us that we are incapable of being consistently faithful to God. Israel could never achieve this throughout her entire history, despite what God had done for her. And none of us should think that we could do any better. So those of us who might think that our lives might be good enough to squeak by on the coming day of judgment should think again! Joel reminds us that it is not those who rely on their own goodness, but rather "everyone who calls on the name of the LORD [who] will be saved" (2:32). And this is the other monumental truth with which Joel comforts us: God's grace and love provide a deliverance that is available to all who simply ask for it.

The prophet tells us that God will make a life-and-death decision for each one of us on the coming day of the Lord. But he gives us the opportunity to make a life-and-death decision ourselves before that time. We can choose what is not life and face a real judgment, or we can choose what is real life and no longer face judgment. We all pass through the valley of decision (3:14), where we decide the ultimate outcome of our lives. Jesus already experienced the judgment of the day of the Lord for those who let him, so they no longer need to fear the day that will come upon those who reject him.

But this is just considering the negative; there is also true life to consider. Just as God lets those who reject him experience now a taste of the judgment that lies in store for them in the future, so he lets those who trust him experience now a taste of the full life that lies in store for them in the future. Those who place their lives in his hands experience peace instead of fear, contentment instead of dissatisfaction, and wholeness instead of brokenness. God's people have set aside a special day each week to remind ourselves of what Jesus has accomplished for us. The day of the Lord is no longer something for us to fear but rather something to celebrate on a day named for it—the Lord's day!

If we are trusting in God's deliverance through Jesus Christ, the prophet Joel reminds us to continue looking to him for true meaning and fulfillment in life. But if we are trusting in ourselves for deliverance, the prophet Joel reminds us that only "darkness and gloom," "clouds and blackness" (2:2) lie ahead, both in this life and when Jesus returns. So let's decide for Jesus while we yet have the opportunity! Let's continue to decide for him every day as we face those things that threaten to weaken our connection to the source of life. Let's make sure those around us realize the decision they are making as well. And let's encourage them, just as Joel encourages us, to find deliverance in the Lord of life from everything that is anti-life.

DISCUSSION QUESTIONS

1. How would you describe the day of the Lord to an unbeliever? How would your description motivate an unbeliever to trust in God? What motivates *you* to trust in God? How does that trust show up in your daily life?

2. Joel describes God as the source of abundant life. Have you come to know that life in your own experience? If not, what might be getting in the way? What steps could you take to enhance your relationship with the source of life?

3. How do you respond to troubles or difficulties in your life? Do you regard them as God's punishment or as opportunities to refocus your life on the only One who does not change and is always reliable? How might you use those experiences to encourage others to trust God?

4. Joel tells God's people after the judgment of the day of the Lord has been experienced, "Do not be afraid … be glad and rejoice" (2:21). Do you still live in fear of the coming day of the Lord? What motivates your actions: fear, or gratitude and joy? If fear, what might be the source of it? How could you live in joy instead?

AMOS

Once we squeegee Joel's locusts off our windshield, we're ready to head down the road to the next Minor Prophet on our itinerary: the prophet Amos. Unfortunately, we soon discover that Amos is not what one would call a warm person. He is not happy at all with how God's people are treating each other. The economy is booming, and both Israel and Judah are enjoying a time of relative freedom. But instead of prompting gratitude and service to God, somehow these blessings have led the people to forget some important truths. Their relationship with God has grown cold. And their relationship with one another has taken a backseat to their own comfort and self-promotion. How could these people who are supposed to be representing God to the world be representing instead behaviors and attitudes that are just the opposite of his? Amos is feeling the burn of righteous indignation. And he's going to read God's people the riot act. Maybe this gruff spokesman for

God has something to say to us as well. Let's park here for a little while to watch the fireworks.

LITTLE-KNOWN FACTS ABOUT AMOS

1. Amos is an outsider.

That Amos receives an unenthusiastic welcome from the people to whom he prophesies is not all that surprising when you think about it. There is nothing about him that would cause anyone to take notice. He isn't even named after anyone famous—his name is found nowhere else in the Bible. He does not have inside connections to the royal court like Isaiah or Zephaniah. Nor is he descended from a priestly family like Jeremiah or Ezekiel. Amos's qualifications as a prophet are even suspect. He himself admits, "I was neither a prophet nor the son of a prophet, but I was a shepherd, and I also took care of sycamore-fig trees. But the LORD took me from tending the flock and said to me, 'Go, prophesy to my people Israel'" (Amos 7:14–15).

So let's be clear: Amos is not even a citizen of the northern kingdom to which he was prophesying! And the town he does come from in the southern kingdom of Judah is insignificant. Amos is from Tekoa, a small town about six miles south of Bethlehem, residing on a stony elevation between two steep valleys descending to the Dead Sea.[1] The situation would be similar to a pastor from rural Iowa with no seminary training traveling to a provincial capital in Canada to tell them what they are doing wrong! We can well understand why the people of Israel were not tripping over themselves in their haste to heed his words. No doubt they wished this hidden prophet would do a better job at staying hidden!

2. Amos's sermons are politically incorrect.

We need to be honest: Amos's personality does not compensate for his lack of credentials. He tells it like it is, without too much in the way of rhetorical niceties. For Amos, the Lord doesn't suggest or cajole; he *roars* (1:2; 3:8). And Amos doesn't simply communicate the Lord's displeasure, he conveys the Lord's *hate*—his hate for Israel's religious festivals, assemblies, and pride (5:21; 6:8). That God should actually hate what his people are doing, even doing on his behalf, is almost incomprehensible, but Amos takes it even further. He lets them know that the God to whom their hollow worship is directed will keep his eye on them for harm and not good (9:4)!

This sermonic style hardly wins Amos any points among his hearers. And certainly, if he *had* gone to seminary, he would have learned an entirely different homiletical approach! But Amos goes beyond simply delivering uncomfortable reports of God's attitude toward his people's behavior; he further transgresses the bounds of political correctness by describing the elite among his hearers in a most disrespectful and disparaging way. He refers to the pampered but pitiless women as *cows*:

Hear this word, you cows of Bashan on Mount
Samaria,

you women who oppress the poor and crush
the needy
and say to your husbands, "Bring us some
drinks!" (4:1)

And the "notable men" fare little better. Amos accuses them of a callous disregard for the fate of their nation, as long as their selfish desires for luxury and abundance are being satisfied:

You drink wine by the bowlful
and use the finest lotions,
but you do not grieve over the ruin of
Joseph. (6:6)

It was already a lot to expect that this outsider would receive a hearing at all. We can only imagine the response his actual words provoked. Only one response, possibly fatal for Amos, is recorded for us in Scripture (see little-known fact 7 below). Any good Israelite career counselor would have advised Amos to keep his day job.

3. Amos may be the first of the "writing prophets."

The Bible refers to many more prophets than those who have left us biblical books. For example, there is no biblical book of Ahijah (1 Kings 11:29) or a book of Huldah (2 Kings 22:14–20). We don't even know the names of some biblical prophets, such as the one hundred prophets of the Lord whom Obadiah hid in two caves

(1 Kings 18:4). Unlike these, the writing prophets are those who *have* left us biblical books. Among this much smaller group, Amos may very well be the first in chronological order (though not in canonical order). This distinction is based on a date for the book of Amos of around 760 BC. This date is arrived at by associating the phrase "two years before the earthquake" found in the opening verse of Amos's prophecy with archaeological evidence at Hazor, which "shows evidence of destruction caused by a great earthquake, traces of which have also been uncovered in archaeological work at Samaria."[2] And that "great earthquake" occurred around 760 BC.

Also, the first verse of Amos's book lists Uzziah as the king of Judah. Uzziah's son, Jotham, began to reign with him in 750 BC. Therefore, the lack of any mention of the coregency of Jotham suggests a time for Amos's prophecy before 750 BC, thus giving him pride of place among the writing prophets.

As we'll see just below, Amos's prophetic ministry may have overlapped that of a few other writing prophets, but he probably takes the prize for being the very first one to make it to press.

4. Amos may be a contemporary of at least three other prophets.

Ancient Jewish sources "speak of the four contemporary prophets Hosea, Amos, Isaiah, and Micah. The last-named prophet, however, was a younger contemporary of the other three."[3] Apart from the unique issues surrounding the dating of Isaiah, this accords reasonably well with modern scholarship, which has calculated the ministries of these prophets as follows:[4]

Amos	~760	
Hosea	750————	—720
Isaiah	740————	—700
Micah	730–?	

The only other prophet who could potentially be added to this list of contemporaries would be Jonah. But the book of Jonah is extremely difficult to date, and so that prophet's inclusion into this group of contemporaries must remain tentative.

5. Amos may have had a speech impediment.

Among the Jewish legends surrounding the prophet Amos, scholar Louis Ginzberg includes a detail not found in Scripture: "Though he [i.e., Amos] had an impediment in his speech, he obeyed the call of God, and betook himself to Beth-el to proclaim to the sinful inhabitants thereof the Divine message with which he had been charged."[5]

This legend receives further support from an expanded description of Isaiah's call (6:8), also found in Jewish texts: "He [i.e., Isaiah] was in his study when he heard a heavenly voice proclaim: 'Whom shall I send? I sent Amos, and they (Israel) said: "God found no better messenger than this stammerer."'"[6]

6. Amos has his own holiday too!

On the calendar of feasts and fasts for the Greek Orthodox Church, Amos's feast day is June 15 (on the Julian calendar, corresponding to June 28 on the modern Gregorian calendar).[7]

In the book of the anniversaries of the martyrs and other saints commemorated by the Roman Catholic Church, the prophet Amos is remembered on March 31.[8]

7. Tradition has it that Amos met a violent end.

Amos does not tell us much about how his sermons were received. The only insight he provides concerning this is found in 7:10–13, and it is not good. Amaziah, the high priest of Bethel, informed the king of Israel (Jeroboam II) that Amos was prophesying against him and Israel—what the high priest described as "raising a conspiracy" (7:10–11). The absence of any response from King Jeroboam at this point in the biblical narrative has been filled in by Jewish tradition, which states:

> The denunciation of the priest Amaziah, of Beth-el, who informed against the prophet before King Jeroboam of Israel, did him no harm, for the king, idolater though he was, entertained profound respect for Amos. He said to himself, "God forbid I should think the prophet guilty of cherishing traitorous plans, and if he were, it would surely be at the bidding of God."[9]

Though the biblical text does not corroborate the king's response to Amos's prophetic activity, it does provide for us the response of the high priest, Amaziah:

Get out, you seer! Go back to the land of Judah. Earn your bread there and do your prophesying there. Don't prophesy anymore at Bethel, because this is the king's sanctuary and the temple of the kingdom. (7:12–13)

So ends the biblical information regarding Amaziah's response. But traditions surrounding his opposition to Amos suggest that matters went much further. These traditions hold that Amaziah tortured him repeatedly and that eventually either he or his son, Ahaziah, mortally wounded Amos by striking him on the temple or piercing his temples with a club or red-hot iron. He was carried, half-dead, back to Tekoa and buried there.[10] Whatever the specific details, the traditions unanimously agree that Amos met a violent end.

THE GOSPEL ACCORDING TO AMOS

Amos shows us our lack of and need for justice and righteousness, both in our relationship with God and in our relationships with one another. He also lays bare for us our congenital inability to pull this off on our own. Jesus came to create a whole different kind of community—a community that is characterized by justice and righteousness and that therefore displays these attributes of God's character. And that is the heart of Amos's message. He does not promote social justice as some sort of vague end in itself. Rather, Amos promotes social justice as a means to intentionally communicate truth about God and the new humanity he is creating through faith in Jesus Christ!

In Jesus Christ, we see what a healthy, intimate relationship with the Father looks like. Jesus lived to do the Father's will (John 4:34; 6:38), he spent time in prayer with him (Luke 6:12; 9:28), and he communicated truth about the Father with his words (John 8:26, 28), his actions (John 10:25; 14:9), and even his emotions (Luke 19:41; John 2:13–17). And in Jesus, we also see how a human being should live in relationship with other human beings: compassionately (Matthew 9:36; 14:14), self-sacrificially (Mark 10:45), and honestly (John 1:14; 14:6). These two relationships—with the Father and with one another—are intimately related. When our relationship with the Father is healthy, our relationships with one another will also be healthy.

But the good news is that Jesus doesn't just demonstrate these relational desiderata *to* us; he actually makes them possible *for* us! He lives his life in perfect unity with the Father so that all who unite with him by faith have that unity with the Father secured for them forever. And by faith in Jesus Christ, we are all welcomed into a new humanity. This new humanity is characterized by different goals and motivations than the old one. It is a humanity made possible by Jesus and achieved by the transforming work of the Spirit. We no longer have to live in the every-man-for-himself world of Amos's day characterized by disrespect for human dignity (Amos 2:6–8), unrest and oppression (3:9), emptiness and futility (4:6–11), slavery to unsatisfying indulgence (6:4–6), and evil times (5:13). We can choose instead the new humanity held out for us through faith in Jesus Christ. When we do, we'll know life as rich as it was intended to be, in fellowship with God and one another. That's the gospel of Amos.

WHY AMOS SHOULD MATTER TO YOU

Amos shows us what life is like when we turn away from God, and it's not a pretty picture. We become like what we worship. The sad truth was that, instead of worshipping the Lord of life, God's people had turned to empty, meaningless idols. They then experienced the inevitable consequence. Their lives had become just as empty and meaningless as the idols they worshipped. This tragic reality manifested itself in corruption instead of justice, oppression instead of encouragement, and callousness instead of compassion. Doesn't this sound all too similar to our contemporary situation? The book of Amos should matter to us because it serves as a reminder of the life we left behind and as a motivation toward the true life God wants for us through faith in Jesus Christ.

God wants us to experience life (John 10:10), life as its very creator designed it to be: full, satisfying, and generative. God's people in Amos's day had exchanged this life for one that seemed to promise something better but epically failed to deliver. Israel was supposed to be a beacon to other nations, showing them the way to true life. Instead, Israel had been duped into adopting the worldview of those who had chosen the illusory over the real; consequently, their society was falling apart. We might be tempted at this point to wag our fingers at Israel. How could they have been so dense? And yet, if we're honest with ourselves, we have to admit that Israel's failings in this regard too often parallel our own.

There is always the temptation for God's people to sidle by degrees into the perspectives and practices of those who have rejected God. After all, such people are always in the majority! But Amos reminds us of the terrible consequences of doing so. When we reject God, we are rejecting everything that gives life meaning, purpose, direction, significance, and security. Human beings are made in God's image; we are made to be like him. When we reject him, we are rejecting our very identity, and nothing but hollow meaninglessness remains.

But when we choose life through faith in Jesus Christ, we experience the new humanity that is part of the new creation (2 Corinthians 5:17). This new humanity, unsurprisingly, will begin to take on the characteristics of God himself: compassion, mercy, and justice. Our complex social interactions will have different motivations and different goals from those of people who are still groping about in the darkness. We will be displaying to the world a different option for life than the miserable one they know. We'll be showing them where the meaning they are desperately searching for can be found. And this new life in Jesus Christ will not only benefit unbelievers by showing them the way to wholeness, but we also will be blessed by it. As a redeemed people being transformed by the radical work of the Holy Spirit, we will inescapably begin to reflect God's character more and more in the way we interact with one another. In other words, we will come to know more fully what it is to be truly human. And that's because we will be doing nothing less than fulfilling our original design function. We will be bearing God's image (Genesis 1:26).

DISCUSSION QUESTIONS

1. God's people were not being a light to the nations. They were not showing unbelievers truth about God as an alternative to the only humanity those nations knew. Amos excoriates God's people for this. What would the prophet say to God's people today? Can unbelievers see God's compassion, mercy, and justice by your behavior? How would someone describe God if they had only you, his representative, to go by? Would they see an alternative way to live as a human being by looking at your life?

2. How might you have given false testimony about God's character to others by the way you have lived? How might you modify your behavior to better communicate truth about your God?

3. Like the people of Amos's day, sometimes we give more focus to form than substance. We get caught up in *doing* things instead of *being* the people God wants us to be. Do you regard "social justice" this way? When you hear the term "social justice," do you think more about things you must do or about how you should be as one being conformed to the likeness of Christ?

4. Even when we think more about *being* than *doing*, we can miss the mark if we try to become different people in our own strength. Are you relying on the power of the Holy Spirit to transform you from the inside out? In what practical ways can you do this?

5. Do your interactions with others, and even God, flow out of a grateful heart, or are you still looking to your good deeds to somehow earn points with God?

6. How would you explain the message of the book of Amos to someone else?

OBADIAH

After leaving fiery Amos behind, we make our way toward the next Minor Prophet: Obadiah. We find him facing southeast, delivering a stinging message concerning Judah's neighbor Edom, located across the Rift Valley below the Dead Sea. The inhabitants of this ancient kingdom were descendants of Esau, Jacob's twin brother. One would therefore expect some familial affection between Judah and Edom, but such is not the case. An (unnamed) foreign nation had attacked Judah, and the Edomites, instead of coming to their relatives' assistance, had actually joined in the abuse. They had kicked Judah when she was down. But disrespecting God's people is regarded by God as disrespecting him (Genesis 12:3). So there was going to be a reckoning for Edom—a reckoning that would prefigure the final reckoning for all those who oppose God and his people.

We'll extend our stay in this short prophecy to see what will come of Edom and what the implications of this drama may be for those of us who are looking on.

LITTLE-KNOWN FACTS ABOUT OBADIAH

1. Obadiah is another mysterious prophet.

We aren't told where he lived, who his father was, how he was regarded, where he died, or where he is buried. We aren't even sure when he prophesied. We also don't know where he was born, though *Lives of the Prophets* 9:1 records a tradition that "Obadiah was from the district of Shechem, of the countryside of Bethacharam."[1] We would welcome any such light into Obadiah's mysterious personal circumstances, but the fact remains that the Bible provides no explicit information.

2. Obadiah has left us the shortest book in the Old Testament.

At only twenty-one verses long, Obadiah checks in as the shortest book of the Old Testament by far. In fact, it is the third shortest book in the entire Bible. The only two books shorter are 2 John (thirteen verses) and 3 John (fourteen verses). The book of Obadiah is so short that the prophet has been (mis)characterized as "the least important prophet."[2] But we remind ourselves once again that *brief* does not mean "unimportant" and that the "Minor" Prophets are called that simply because of their brevity and not because of their significance.

3. It may sound unusual to us, but Obadiah was a common name in Old Testament times.

Obadiah is a common name in the Old Testament. In fact, there may be as many as a dozen people with that name, though it is difficult to give a precise count because some of the scattered references may be referring to the same person. We find an Obadiah in

- 1 Kings 18:3–16 (the palace administrator in King Ahab's court);
- 1 Chronicles 3:21 (a descendant of King Jehoiachin, born after his exile to Babylon);
- 1 Chronicles 7:3 (a descendant of Jacob's son Issachar);
- 1 Chronicles 8:38 and 9:44 (a descendant of King Saul);
- 1 Chronicles 9:16 (one of the Levites who was among those who were "the first to resettle on their own property in their own towns" [1 Chronicles 9:2] after the exile);
- 1 Chronicles 12:9 (the second in command among the Gadites who defected to David's side in his conflict with King Saul);

- 1 Chronicles 27:19 (the father of Ishmaiah, the leader of the tribe of Zebulun early in the reign of King David);
- 2 Chronicles 17:7 (one of the officials of King Jehoshaphat of Judah who were sent to teach the Law of God in the towns of Judah);
- 2 Chronicles 34:12 (a Levite descended from Merari who oversaw the repair and restoration of the temple under King Josiah);
- Ezra 8:9 (one of the descendants of Joab who traveled with Ezra from Babylon back to Jerusalem after the exile);
- Nehemiah 10:5 (one of the priests among the returned exiles who, along with Nehemiah, affixed their seals to a binding agreement to follow the Law of God [the same person who is mentioned in Ezra 8:9?]); and
- Nehemiah 12:25 (one of the "gatekeepers who guarded the storerooms at the gates" during the days of Nehemiah and Ezra [the same person who is mentioned in Ezra 8:9 and Nehemiah 10:5?]).

That Obadiah should be a common name is not surprising when we learn that the name means "servant of the LORD." There is no doubt that this would be a popular name among devout Israelites, or at least among those who wanted their sons to be considered as such.

4. It is possible that the prophet Obadiah worked in King Ahab's royal court.

Although most scholars argue that none of these other individuals can be identified as the prophet Obadiah,[3] there are those who at least allow for the possibility that the prophet Obadiah is the same person who is described in 1 Kings 18:3–16 as the palace administrator of King Ahab.[4] Strong support for this conclusion is found in widespread Jewish tradition, which holds that these are, in fact, the same person.[5]

The tradition identifying Ahab's palace administrator with Obadiah the prophet is elaborate and interweaves with narratives concerning Elijah, Elisha, King Ahab, and Ahab's son Joram. The traditional lore begins with an account of a selfless and heroic act on the part of Obadiah. When Jezebel was carrying out her campaign to exterminate the Lord's prophets, Obadiah the prophet (tradition has it) was the same Obadiah who hid one hundred prophets of the Lord in two caves and supplied them with food and water (1 Kings 18:4). Another tradition records that Obadiah's provision for these prophets required him to take out a loan, on which Ahab's son Joram "exacted a high rate of interest."[6] When Obadiah died, the tradition continues, the king sought to hold Obadiah's children responsible for this debt their father had incurred. Obadiah's desperate wife went to the grave of her husband and cried out to her deceased husband for help. In some mysterious and unspecified way, Obadiah, so the tradition goes, told her to take the last bit of oil she had remaining and to go to Elisha to ask him to intercede with God on Obadiah's behalf. The deceased Obadiah explained that God would certainly provide for her inasmuch as God had incurred a debt of his own to Obadiah:

> "For God," he said, "is my debtor, seeing that I pro-
> vided a hundred prophets, not only with bread and
> water, but also with oil to illuminate their hiding-
> place, for do not the Scriptures say: 'He that hath
> pity upon the poor lendeth unto the Lord'?"[7]

By this means, therefore, Jewish tradition links the events recounted in 2 Kings 4:1–7 with the prophet Obadiah. In the biblical account, a widow "of a man from the company of the prophets" was being dunned by a creditor who was seeking payment for a debt incurred by her deceased husband. The widow sought help from Elisha, who miraculously provided her with oil to pay her debts and to take care of herself and her sons.

The parallels drawn by the Jewish traditions above are clear. The widow "of a man from the company of prophets," asserts the tradition, is none other than the widow of the prophet Obadiah![8]

To review, these various elements of connected traditions, though relatively insubstantial on their own, converge to strengthen the hypothesis that the prophet Obadiah was, in fact, the same Obadiah who was the palace administrator in King Ahab's court:

- The prophet and the palace administrator have the same name.

- The palace administrator was a devout believer in the Lord (as no doubt was the prophet).
- The palace administrator went against the king's command by hiding one hundred prophets of the Lord (suggesting also that he had some special access to these prophets, perhaps because he too was a prophet).
- The prophet Elijah respected the palace administrator, as he would if the official were a fellow prophet.[9]

Of course, none of these traditions has the benefit of biblical corroboration. Then again, none of them is excluded by biblical revelation either. For now, it seems reasonable at least to allow for the possibility that the prophet Obadiah was in the difficult position of serving in the court of an Israelite king whose queen was seeking to eradicate prophets like him.

5. A seal bearing the name of Obadiah has been found.

Seals were used for impressing the names of their owners on various items, including blobs of clay (called bullae) that were used to seal letters and documents. One of these seals has been found bearing this inscription: "(Belonging) to Obadyahu, servant of the king."[10] Obadyahu is simply a variant, fuller spelling of the name Obadiah. This Obadiah may be none other than the palace administrator of King Ahab mentioned in 1 Kings 18:3, who, as we have seen, might be the prophet Obadiah. Imagine, a seal used by the prophet Obadiah himself might actually have survived to this day!

6. Jewish tradition suggests that Obadiah himself was of Edomite ancestry!

One fascinating tradition suggests that our Obadiah is a descendant of Eliphaz the Temanite, who is one of Job's friends (Job 2:11).[11] The name Teman is listed as a descendant of Esau in early genealogies (Genesis 36:11, 15, 42), and Esau and Edom were interchangeable names (Genesis 25:30; 36:1, 8, 19). In later history, Teman became associated with the area of Edom more generally (Jeremiah 49:20; Ezekiel 25:13). If this tradition is true, then not only is Obadiah not an Israelite, but he would also be prophesying against his own people, the Edomites! No wonder there is a Jewish tradition of the heavenly council providing divine encouragement for Obadiah to do just that.[12]

If Obadiah were, in fact, an Edomite and was called to be a prophet of the Lord, he would have had to become a proselyte to Judaism at some point. Jewish tradition finds support for that conclusion by noting that Obadiah is described by the author of 1 Kings as "a devout believer in the LORD" (18:3). The Hebrew words being translated here are יָרֵא אֶת־יְהֹוָה מְאֹד (*yārē' 'et-yhwh me'ōd*) and can be woodenly translated as "one greatly fearing the Lord." A "Lord fearer" or, more generally, a "God fearer" was in later Jewish history the usual name for a convert to Judaism. So the application of this term to Obadiah suggests, according to tradition, that he too was a convert to Judaism and not a Jew by birth.[13] But he is not just any convert! His legendary "charity and lovingkindness" earn him a place in tradition alongside such stars of the faith as Abraham, Joseph, and Job.[14] In fact, Obadiah occupies such a lofty place in Jewish tradition that he is regarded as the overseer of the first division of Paradise, in which "dwell the proselytes who embraced Judaism of their own free will, not from compulsion."[15]

7. Obadiah's entire prophecy is "about Edom."

Apart from the book of Nahum, the book of Obadiah is the only other biblical book focused entirely on a foreign nation. But what do we know about this nation that gets such special attention that it warrants its own biblical book? Surprisingly, what we know about the nation of Edom is very limited. While perhaps overstating the case a bit, one commentator goes so far as to say, "All the monuments and written records of the Edomites have perished, so what information can be obtained about them comes from the writings of their neighbors and enemies, the Israelites, Egyptians, Assyrians, and Babylonians, and from archaeological exploration."[16] Let's explore some of the meager information these resources offer us.

The biblical materials inform us that the nation located on the southeastern border of Judah is known by two names that are each related to Esau, the brother of Jacob. The most common name is Edom (אֱדוֹם 'ĕdôm), which is very similar to the Hebrew word for *red* (אָדֹם 'ādōm). In Genesis 25, the word "red" is related to Esau in two ways: We read in verse 30 that because Esau asked for *red* stew when he came in from the open country, "that is why he was also called Edom." But the color red is associated with Esau even earlier in the narrative. Verse 25 shows that when Esau was born, he was red. Red was also the color of the rocks and soil of the land later occupied by the Edomites.[17]

The nation of Edom is also "often closely connected with the land of Seir or Mount Seir … Seir (meaning 'rough,' 'hairy') referring to the wooded eastern slopes of the Wadi Araba."[18] A play on this name connects Seir (שֵׂעִיר *śēʿîr*) back to the account in Genesis 25, where we read concerning Esau's birth, "his whole body was like a hairy [שֵׂעָר *śēʿār*] garment" (25:25).

We have no extrabiblical resources that provide details regarding the origin of the nation of Edom. The surviving references to Edom indicate an already-established nation. The first mention of the alternative designation for Edom (Seir) occurs in Egyptian references dating to the fourteenth to the twelfth century BC. The first actual mention of Edom occurs in a late thirteenth-century BC letter "from a frontier official to his superior."[19] Edom seems to have continued to exist for a few decades after Judah was conquered by the Babylonians in 586 BC. The evidence points to the end of the nation of Edom coming at around 552 BC, during a military campaign of Nabonidus, the last ruler of the Neo-Babylonian Empire.[20] After a period of desolation following Edom's demise, its land was subsequently repopulated by the Nabataeans, a nomadic Arabic tribe.[21]

Another piece of information provided by the biblical sources is that Edom had a reputation for wisdom.[22] In fact, in one of the biblical wisdom books, both Job and his "friend," Eliphaz the Temanite, were Edomites! Job lived in "the land of Uz" (Job 1:1), an area paralleling Edom in Lamentations 4:21. Eliphaz hailed from Teman (Job 2:11), a term paralleling Edom in Jeremiah 49:20.[23]

The Bible records virtually unending conflict between Edom and Judah during the period of the monarchy.[24] Because of this seemingly interminable hostility between Edom and Judah, it is difficult to assign a date with absolute certainty to the particular historical occasion giving rise to Obadiah's prophecy. The most likely time seems to be the weeks and months surrounding the Babylonian destruction of Judah and Jerusalem in 586 BC.[25] It was Edom's unseemly and opportunistic behavior toward Judah during this period that would have provoked Obadiah's prophetic rebuke. It is also this age-old clash between Edom and Jacob's descendants that ultimately led to the name Edom being used symbolically to stand for all those who oppose God's people.[26]

8. Obadiah has his own holiday too!

Obadiah is remembered with a feast day (November 19 on the Julian calendar and December 2 on the modern Gregorian calendar) on the liturgical calendar of the Greek Orthodox Church.[27]

THE GOSPEL ACCORDING TO OBADIAH

Unsurprisingly, God fulfilled his terrible promise to Edom. They were ultimately destroyed, most probably by the Babylonian king Nabonidus around 552 BC. But the implications of Obadiah's message outlive Edom, because Edom's fate also represents the ultimate fate of all those who set themselves against God and his people.[28] Obadiah hints at this in verses 15 and 16, where he associates what will happen to Edom with what will happen to "all nations." To whom does this term "all nations" refer? The bad news, the "anti-gospel," is that it refers to every human being!

The uncomfortable truth is that we are all guilty of the sins of Edom. We all have prideful hearts (verse 3). We all trust in people (verse 7) or things (verse 6) rather than God. We all like to think of ourselves as morally superior to those who are experiencing hardship of one sort or another (verse 12). We all can be arrogant and inhumane. We all deserve God's righteous vengeance. And every human being will, in fact, experience that divine vengeance. This will happen in only one of two possible ways. Either we will continue to oppose God and his people and experience God's vengeance directly. Or—and here is the good news—we can put our faith in Jesus as our representative. Jesus is the only human being who doesn't deserve God's wrath but who nevertheless experienced every bit of it on our behalf. When we put our faith in Jesus, the divine vengeance he experienced on the cross is credited as our experience as well. This is powerfully welcome good news!

There is indeed gospel in Obadiah, but it might not be where we first look for it. At first glance, the book of Obadiah looks like nothing but bad news. But we can find the good news hidden behind our condemnation of Edom's opposition to God and his people. Only when we are able to see that our condemnation of Edom's attitude and actions is, in fact, also a condemnation of ourselves do we begin to look for the lifeline of good news that God is holding out to us. That lifeline, Obadiah tells us, is on Mount Zion (verse 17). In other words, our deliverance must come from God himself. And God has indeed provided that deliverance by sending his own Son to accomplish the task. Jesus took upon himself that divine condemnation of sin and all its horrible consequences, deserved by both Edom and all of us, so that everyone who trusts in him will never have to experience that condemnation firsthand.

WHY OBADIAH SHOULD MATTER TO YOU

Trusting in Jesus not only ensures we will never experience the wrath of God (because Jesus has already done that for us), but it also initiates within us a counter-Edom transformation.

The Edomites believed they had the right to do what they did. They had historically been dominated by Judah, and now it was time for Judah to suffer Edom's outrage. They were going to take justice into their own hands.

The problem, of course, with any of us exacting justice ourselves is that we always have only a very small window through which to view what is a much larger picture. So we end up basing our desired vengeance on extremely limited data. Also, our ability to be just in dispensing the vengeance we deem appropriate is hampered by our own sin-contaminated motives. Our pride, our sense of entitlement, and our selfishness grossly distort our perspective. There is, in actual fact, only One who is capable of seeing the entire picture and who is unimpeded by sin. That's why God tells us to leave vengeance to him. He alone knows the best way and time to bring resolution to injustice. He says, "It is mine to avenge; I will repay" (Deuteronomy 32:35).

God has already exercised his mighty vengeance upon all of us who have put our faith in Jesus Christ. And how incredibly lovingly and graciously he has done it! He sent his own Son to stand in our place and experience that vengeance for us. By our faith in Christ, God has, in fact, destroyed us. He has literally caused us to cease to exist. But he has done this by making us entirely new creations in Christ (2 Corinthians 5:17)! This is the kind of vengeance we should want for everyone who opposes God and his people. The choice is clear. If we want other people to experience, as we have, God's new-creation-producing, new-life-generating vengeance instead of remaining in their old-creation, life-draining, self-centered existence, then what Obadiah says should indeed matter to us.

DISCUSSION QUESTIONS

1. Through Obadiah, God tells us that the Edomites had mistakenly put their confidence in their seemingly impregnable homes in the mountains, in their alliances, in their wisdom, and in their military. All of these would prove to be false confidences. In what might *you* have mistakenly put your confidence instead of in God?

2. The Edomites thought it was appropriate to pay back those they felt had wronged them. What, if anything, do you think is wrong with that?

3. Do you see any connection between the vengeance of God that "all the nations will drink continually" (Obadiah verse 16) and the

cup filled with the wine of God's wrath that Jesus prayed about to the Father in Gethsemane (Matthew 26:42)?

4. If you used the same standard to judge yourself that you use to judge other people, how would you measure up? Would you end up experiencing the same fate you have deemed appropriate for others?

JONAH

We leave the book of Obadiah with a renewed appreciation for Judah's righteous indignation at the callousness of the Edomites, their own relatives. So when we learn that the next prophet on our journey through this hidden biblical neighborhood will address the Assyrians, we anticipate a similar prophetic denunciation. In fact, we expect the judgment to be much, much worse

because the Assyrians have no familial ties to Israel. Not only that, but the Assyrians were ruthless, vicious, and universally feared. They committed unspeakable atrocities against any nation that dared to stand in their way. Surely the judge of all the earth would dispatch Jonah to announce the welcome end of these people! How surprising, then, to find in this book not a condemnation of the Assyrians but an extension of God's compassion toward them! If God could be compassionate toward people like this, then there seems to be no end to his mercy. Isn't that a good thing? Then why does it leave such a bitter taste in our mouths? That's a question we'll have to put to the prophet Jonah. But when we pull into town, we learn that we've just missed him. He shipped out on a fast boat to Tarshish. We'll follow the news clips concerning him preserved in this prophetic book as we seek to excavate the truth we're intended to discover hidden underneath the layers of Jonah's self-righteousness, selfishness, and disobedience.

LITTLE-KNOWN FACTS ABOUT JONAH

1. We can't be certain that Jonah even wrote the book that is named after him!

It should be noted at the outset that the book of Jonah is technically anonymous. It begins with the words "The word of the LORD came to Jonah," not with "The word of the LORD came to *me*." The book is therefore predominantly a third-person account of the misadventures of a reluctant prophet and not firsthand memoirs from the prophet's own hand.

An exception to this is the prayer of Jonah that comprises the bulk of chapter 2. Only here and in a few other passages distributed throughout the book (1:9, 12; 3:4; 4:2–3, 8, 9) do we have a record of Jonah's own words delivered in the first person. But all of these could simply be recollections of the prophet's words recorded for us by a later biographer, one who unfortunately remains unidentified.

2. We know more about Jonah than any of the previous Minor Prophets.

The books of Hosea and Joel provide the names of those prophets' fathers. The book of Amos informs us of the name of his hometown. But the Bible provides both of those pieces of information for Jonah. He is the son of Amittai (Jonah 1:1), who hails from Gath Hepher (2 Kings 14:25). Gath Hepher was a small, otherwise unremarkable border town in the territory of Zebulun (Joshua 19:13). There Jonah was born, and there, if tradition is to be believed, is his tomb—or at least very close by in the current Arab village of el-Meshed.[1]

The fact that a prophecy of Jonah is mentioned in 2 Kings 14:25 as the grounds or motivation of the territorial expansion of Jeroboam II (793–753 BC) enables us to conclude that Jonah ministered at or before that time.[2]

The book of Jonah also provides us with much more insight into the prophet's internal landscape than we have been given for previous Minor Prophets. We see his awareness of his guilt in running away from God (Jonah 1:12). Within his piscatorial precincts, we see Jonah's distress (2:2), his hope for deliverance (2:4), and his gratitude for God's salvation (2:9). When the Ninevites repent, we see Jonah's petulance and virtual tantrum when God then extends his compassion toward them (4:1, 3)—an extreme disgruntlement that subsequently transfers to something as innocuous as a plant (4:8–9).

So far we have been on fairly solid ground, but our footing becomes increasingly less certain when we step away from the biblical materials to the legendary. Nevertheless, some attention to this traditional lore provides us with tantalizing tidbits of detail. For example, one line of tradition pulls the time of Jonah's life back to the days of Elijah (the first half of the ninth century BC). This widespread tradition identifies Jonah as the son of the widow of Zarephath. Jonah would therefore be this son who died and was raised to life by Elijah (1 Kings 17:7–24)! Even Jerome utilized this midrashic tradition in his commentary on Jonah, associating the widow's final word to Elijah (אֱמֶת *'ĕmet* truth) with Jonah's ancestry (אֲמִתַּי *'ămittay* Amittai).[3] *Lives of the Prophets* 10:6 adds that this resuscitation of Jonah by Elijah not only answered the prayer of the bereaved mother but also demonstrated to Jonah "that it is not possible to run away from God"[4]—even apparently by death!

Another tradition asserts that Jonah was a disciple of Elisha (the second half of the ninth century BC) and that the "man from the company of the prophets" whom Elisha charged with the task of anointing Jehu as king of Israel (2 Kings 9:1–10) was none other than Jonah himself.[5]

Finally, a couple of traditions suggest not only that Jonah was married, but also that his wife was renowned for her upright character. According to these traditions, the name of Jonah's wife was Yoam, the daughter of Azen.[6] She was widely admired for taking upon herself the difficulty of making pilgrimages to Jerusalem, something a woman was not required to do. Indeed, it was during one of these pilgrimages, so the tradition goes, that the prophetic Spirit first descended upon her husband, Jonah.[7]

3. There are questions regarding whether the book of Jonah is historical.

Several objections are often raised against the historicity of the events recorded in the book of Jonah—or against the notion that the book was ever intended to be read as historical. These include the entire episode of the huge fish, the use of the title "king of Nineveh" instead of the historically accurate "king of Assyria," the description of the size of Nineveh, and the inclusion of animals in Nineveh's repentance. Let's consider each one of these separately.

The first and perhaps most frequent objection to the historicity of the book of Jonah is the "huge fish" and Jonah's extended, conscious stay within it. One must allow that a God who could fashion a huge fish to swallow Jonah (1:17) could surely also preserve Jonah within it.

Recourse to accounts of other sailors who have managed to survive for a period of time within a large fish is entirely unnecessary. It is only an exclusion of the miraculous that could leave a reader or hearer flummoxed over this detail.

Another objection to the book's historicity centers on its reference to the "king of Nineveh." The argument asserts that this unnamed king (unusual in itself) should be referred to as the "king of Assyria." It is noted that "neither biblical nor Assyrian sources ever refer to the king of Assyria as the king of Nineveh."[8] A related issue is that the book of Jonah "seems to operate under the assumption that Nineveh is the capital of Assyria. This, however, would not have been the case during Jonah's time.... Nineveh did not become the capital of the Neo-Assyrian Empire until Sennacherib relocated the center of his government there at the end of the eighth century BC, some forty-five years after the period of Jonah's ministry under Jeroboam II of Israel."[9] But two factors mitigate this objection. First, the term "king of Nineveh" may, in fact, not be referring to the king of Assyria but to a governor or noble who was ruling over the city or province of Nineveh. Second, there is linguistic evidence that the term "king" could indeed refer to governors or nobles who ruled over more localized regions.[10]

A third objection to the historicity of the book of Jonah is its allusion to the great size of Nineveh. In Jonah 3:3, we read that "it took three days to go through it." First, it should be pointed out that "three days" can mean anything from one day and a part of the days before and after (that is, just over twenty-four hours) to a full seventy-two hours. Second, three days could refer to the time required to complete the project (including visits to city gates, the palace, temple courtyards, and other public places) rather than the time required to walk through or around the city. Alternatively, three days could refer to the time required to travel through the province of Nineveh, not simply the city of Nineveh proper.[11]

A final objection to the historicity of the book of Jonah is the alleged unusual inclusion of animals in the Ninevites' repentance rituals. Specifically, isn't it strange that the king of Nineveh would direct not only people but also animals to "be covered with sack-cloth" (Jonah 3:8)? But this is surely the weakest of the objections. Even today, horses used in funeral processions are often arrayed in specialized mourning tack.

Finally, that the book was not intended to be read as a historical account might be suggested by the fact that Jonah is the only character in the book with a name and by the apparent effort to strip the narrative of other "historical details in order to highlight the universality of the book's message and to facilitate its appropriation by succeeding generations of God's people."[12] Of course, this argument is an argument from silence. One can hardly offer a lack of data as proof of anything.

One might argue for the historicity of the book by pointing to Jesus's references to Jonah and the Ninevites (Matthew 12:39–41; Luke 11:29–32). But this argument is countered by claims that Jesus was simply making his point by referring to a well-known character from a popular story rather than to an actual historical figure—much like a preacher using a character from film or literature to make a point in a sermon.

Though, as we have seen, there are reasonable counterarguments for every argument levied against the historicity of the book of Jonah, the possibility remains that it was not intended to be read as history but rather as a parable or allegory. And we must also acknowledge that one can hold to the divine authorship of Scripture and still believe the book was not meant to be read as history. The message of the book is the same regardless if it is read as history. Nevertheless, the fact holds that there are no entirely convincing arguments for discounting the historicity of the book. So, apart from compelling reasons to read it otherwise and because there is no question of the historicity of the other Minor Prophets, it seems the wisest course is to regard the book of Jonah as a record of actual, historical events.

4. Jonah is the meanest person in the book!

Apart from God himself, there are relatively few characters in the book of Jonah. In its four short chapters, we encounter Jonah, the sailors, and the Ninevites, including the king of Nineveh. When each of these is considered separately, it is quite surprising to find that it is Jonah, the only Israelite in the book, who appears the least praiseworthy!

The sailors immediately look for divine assistance in the face of their maritime nightmare, but Jonah simply snoozes below decks (1:4–5). When Jonah reveals to them the only solution to their problem—throwing him overboard—they balk and look for any other alternative. They extend such consideration to Jonah even though it is clear, as he himself acknowledges, that he alone is responsible for their catastrophic situation (1:12–13). Even when they finally realize that they have no choice but to follow through with Jonah's recommended course of action, they cry out to the Lord for forgiveness (1:14). And after they do the deed, they sacrifice to the Lord and make vows to him with fear and reverence (1:16).

The Ninevites appear in a favorable light as well. They respond to Jonah's threatened divine judgment with belief, a fast, and visible signs of humble repentance (3:5). No less a figure than the king himself descends from his throne, removes the garments of his royal office, and in humility sits in the dust while clothed in sackcloth (3:6).

The final, and chief, character in the book, the one from whom we expect behavior commensurate with a member of the covenant community, is the only one whose response to God is defiance instead of humility! He runs away from the Lord in bold disobedience to his divinely given commission (1:3). Even worse, Jonah has such a high estimation of his own sense of justice that he considers himself capable of rendering judgment upon God, especially in regard to what he considers God's improper compassion toward the repentant Ninevites (4:1–3)! Jonah is presented so negatively that his last recorded words consist of a narcissistic rant that he would rather die than be uncomfortable (4:8–9). This is hardly a person any of us would hold up as a hero of the faith!

5. Jewish tradition suggests that among the Israelites, Jonah was known as a false prophet!

Perhaps related to the above point is the tradition that Jonah is a false prophet. The first piece of evidence offered to support this view is a prophecy of Jonah not even found in the book of Jonah! It is found instead in 2 Kings 14:25.

Jewish tradition holds that what is recorded in 2 Kings 14:25 is just the end of the story. Jonah, this tradition maintains, had originally received a divine call not to proclaim an expansion of the kingdom under the evil Israelite king Jeroboam, but rather "to proclaim their destruction to the inhabitants of Jerusalem. The doom did not come to pass, because they repented of their wrong-doing, and God had mercy upon them. Among the Israelites Jonah was, therefore, known as 'the false prophet.'" This, the tradition asserts, explains his reluctance to go to Nineveh where he was afraid the same thing would happen again. He would proclaim destruction, the people would repent, God would have mercy upon them and spare them, and Jonah would once again look like a false prophet.[13]

A second piece of evidence comes from the book of Jonah itself. It is certainly true that in the biblical account, Jonah was told to "preach against" Nineveh (Jonah 1:2) and that, after a period of reflection in the huge fish, he proclaimed to them, "Forty more days and Nineveh will be overthrown" (3:4). Of course, that did not happen. If one of the signs of a false prophet is that what he prophesies does not come to pass (Deuteronomy 18:22), then it is understandable that some may well have viewed Jonah as a false prophet.

But Jonah could rightly be considered a false prophet if one believes a prophet communicates truth only through words. The reality is, however, that prophets communicate God's message with their actions and emotions as well. The account of Jonah's behavior and response to his divine calling is intended not to be primarily a story of Nineveh's repentance but a message to Israel about her own behavior and response to her divine calling. And what Jonah was communicating to Israel about these things was certainly not false. It was spot on!

6. The book of Jonah is really a message to Israel.

Jonah, a prophet of Israel, never prophesies to Israel—at least not directly. This made some earlier Jewish scholars a little uneasy. They went so far as to consider the book of Jonah "a book by itself, and not a part of the Book of the Twelve." This assertion was likely made "to call attention to the fact that this biblical book has a character of its own, its contents dealing exclusively with the story of a heathen city."[14]

But Jonah certainly has something to say to the Israelites, although indirectly. He is giving the people of Israel the opportunity to see what they look like. He is acting, in effect, like a one-man nation. They, like Jonah, had run away from their divine calling to bring God's truth to the nations. They had evidenced a desire to hoard God's blessings for themselves, with an attendant unwillingness to allow others to share in them. As we will see more fully a little later, any uneasiness God's people may have with Jonah's untoward behavior may in fact spring from an unpleasant recognition of themselves in this petulant prophet.

7. Jonah's fish has spawned some amazing tales!

It is precisely at the point of our greatest curiosity—what it was like for Jonah inside the great fish—that Jewish tradition has filled the void. We are told, for example, that the fish that swallowed Jonah had been specifically created and designated for him when the world was created. This fish, as it turns out, served Jonah as a well-appointed submersible watercraft:

> [It] was so large that the prophet was as comfortable inside him as in a spacious synagogue. The eyes of the fish served Jonah as windows, and, besides, there was diamond, which shone brilliantly as sun at midday, so that Jonah could see all things in the sea down to its very bottom.... Three days Jonah had spent in the belly of the fish, and he still felt so comfortable that he did not think of imploring God to change his condition.[15]

Clearly, then, something else was going to have to be done to get Jonah into the proper frame of mind.

> God sent a female fish big with three hundred sixty-five thousand little fish to Jonah's host, to demand the surrender of the prophet, else she would swallow both him and the guest he harbored.... So it came about that Jonah was transferred to another abode. His new quarters, which he had to share with all the little fish, were far from comfortable, and from the bottom of his heart a prayer for deliverance arose to God on high. The last words of his long petition were, "I shall redeem my vow," whereupon God commanded the fish to spew Jonah out.[16]

To say that Jonah's new accommodations were "far from comfortable" appears to be a gross understatement. Indeed, the tradition continues, "the intense heat in the belly of the fish had consumed his garments, and made his hair fall out, and he was sore plagued by a swarm of insects."[17] Jonah's baldness and attractiveness to insects caused by the caustic environment of his second aquatic habitat were the reasons, helpfully provided by the tradition though absent in the biblical text, that God caused the plant to grow and provide shade for Jonah as he sat down east of Nineveh to see what would become of the city (Jonah 4:5–6).

Jonah's suffering throughout his entire ordeal was so severe, the tradition concludes, that he joined the ranks of that extremely select group of human beings who have been exempted from death. He was, so we're told, permitted to enter Paradise alive.[18]

8. Jonah has his own holiday too!

On the calendar of feasts and fasts for the Greek Orthodox Church, Jonah's feast day is September 21 (on the Julian calendar, corresponding to October 4 on the modern Gregorian calendar).[19] In the book of the anniversaries of the martyrs and other saints commemorated by the Roman Catholic Church, the prophet Jonah is remembered on September 21 "in the land of Saar."[20]

THE GOSPEL ACCORDING TO JONAH

God sent Jonah to the Assyrians with a message of judgment. But when the Assyrians repented, the "gracious and compassionate God, slow to anger and abounding in love" (Jonah 4:2) extended those attributes toward them and "did not bring on them the destruction he had threatened" (3:10). This was extremely difficult for Jonah to accept. Surely justice required that such a nation, so he reasoned, should be wiped from the face of the earth. If ever there were a nation that deserved God's judgment, this had to be the one. That God would instead show mercy and compassion to them was simply impossible to understand. And in the same way that it was impossible for Jonah to understand, it was impossible for the Israelites to understand.

And we may wholeheartedly agree that it *is*, in fact, impossible to understand! But only in accepting it do we encounter the gospel. By granting his compassion to a nation as loathsome and reprehensible as the Assyrians, God communicates to all of us the limitless range and extent of his mercy. If even the *Assyrians* fall within its scope, then surely we do too, no matter how undeserving we may regard ourselves. Make no mistake; we are *all* undeserving! And yet God's mercy extends to every one of us.

What Jonah and the Israelites he represents had to learn was that they were just as undeserving of God's compassion as were the Assyrians. God, in a way and for a reason impossible for us to understand, extends his love and mercy indiscriminately. Surely the basis for this divine beneficence cannot be the inherent worthiness of its recipients, because every one of us is unworthy. As the apostle Paul reminds us, "All have sinned and fall short of the glory of God" (Romans 3:23). And yet, "God demonstrates his own love for us in this: While we were still sinners, Christ died for us" (Romans 5:8).

And so the disobedience and selfishness of the prophet Jonah, who wanted to limit God's salvation to only those he thought deserved it, find their exact opposites in the obedience and selflessness of Jesus, who gathers the recipients of God's grace and favor from "every nation, tribe, language and people" (Revelation 14:6). This is the hidden gospel of Jonah, and it is indeed good news for all of us who realize in quiet moments of honest reflection that we are no better than the Assyrians. But, praise God, that does not exclude us from his love!

WHY JONAH SHOULD MATTER TO YOU

The book of Jonah should matter to us because it exposes the heart of the gospel and sheds light on the goal of the Christian life. The last verse of the book reverberates with implications. God asks, "Should I not have concern for the great city of Nineveh?" (Jonah 4:11). By means of this question, God reminds us of his expansive love—a love that dares to blanket even those who by all human measure do not deserve to experience its warmth. This is indeed the heart of the gospel, and it convicts us of an attitude that may lie within us that is often far more restrictive. We are more than happy to receive God's gracious salvation for ourselves, but we are often unwilling for others to share in this blessing as well.

God had called his people Israel to be his channel of blessing to the nations (Genesis 12:2–3), a light for the Gentiles (Isaiah 42:6; 49:6). But Israel was more often content to hide that blessing away for themselves than extend it openhandedly to other nations. This stinginess is what Jonah demonstrates to his own people about his own people. He runs away from his calling and is infuriated when God is merciful to those he believes don't deserve it, not realizing that he doesn't either! Jonah evidences less compassion than God, and for this, God rebukes him, Israel, and perhaps even us. Would our response be any less recalcitrant than Jonah's if God called us, for example, to bring his message of salvation to a terrorist cell in Yemen? Probably not.

God has made us to be like him (Genesis 1:26). And God is unmistakably merciful and compassionate. He has done nothing less than send his own Son to suffer and die for our salvation. To be like God, then, is to be just as merciful and compassionate. Jesus brought God's message of salvation to those who mocked him and ultimately crucified him. He calls us to be willing to do the same. As we carry out Jesus's command to take the gospel to "all nations" (Matthew 28:19)—even those who may frighten us or whom we feel don't deserve it—God's compassion will become more evident in our lives and we will become more like Christ.

As the Holy Spirit continues his transforming work within us, we will grow as eager to share the good news of Jesus Christ with others as we are aware of our unworthiness to have received it ourselves. Then, ultimately, the gospel that is hidden away in the account of this hidden prophet will shine forth for all the world to see. That should matter to every grateful child of God.

DISCUSSION QUESTIONS

1. Do you believe that you have somehow merited God's salvation? Are you amazed at God's compassion toward you, or do you think that you deserve it? If you could somehow be worthy of God's compassion, then why would Jesus have had to come?

2. If you could put limits on God's compassion, what would they be? Would those limits ultimately exclude even you? How wide would those limits have to be in order to include you? What does your appreciation for God's compassion say about your understanding of your need for it?

3. Does your enthusiasm in communicating God's compassion to the people around you look more like Jonah's or Jesus's? How was God's compassion communicated to you? How do you think you should be communicating it to others?

4. Do you see parallels between your life and Jonah's? Do you too sometimes refuse to communicate God's love and mercy to other people? Are you doing so even now? Are there particular people to whom you have the most difficult time communicating the good news of God's love? Have you thought about why that is?

5. Although it may be uncomfortable for you, do you go ahead and tell people who are different from you the good news of God's love for them too? What if those people are hostile to you or make fun of you? What did it cost Jesus to communicate God's love to us? What are you willing to give to communicate it to others?

MICAH

Jonah is a biblical tourist destination that still receives a modest amount of traffic. But we soon discover that this is not the case at all for the next book on our journey: Micah. Indeed, if it were not for the quotation of a single verse of Micah's prophecy (5:2) in the gospel of Matthew (2:6), this small biblical book would be in danger of slipping into complete obscurity. Micah is certainly one of the most hidden of the hidden prophets of the Bible. This is true even though he delivers full-throated words of both judgment and hope during times of cataclysmic upheavals for the northern kingdom of Israel and the southern kingdom of Judah. Further minimizing Micah's name recognition is the fact that he is almost totally eclipsed by the rock-star status of his prophetic contemporary, Isaiah. But now it is time for us to bring this hidden prophet out from the shadows and give him his own time in the spotlight. Our brief stay in his canonical borough will no doubt place him back on our biblical maps and add to our growing store of biblical treasures.

LITTLE-KNOWN FACTS ABOUT MICAH

1. Micah ministered in Isaiah's shadow.

In the opening verse of his prophecy, we're told that Micah ministered during the reigns of "Jotham, Ahaz, and Hezekiah, kings of Judah." This would place the outside boundaries of his ministry from 750–686 BC, with the actual period of his work falling somewhere in the middle. His ministry was therefore entirely under the shadow of the more illustrious Isaiah, whose ministry occurred during almost exactly the same period. This fact may explain why almost no extrabiblical traditions exist regarding Micah. It seems as though almost all the creative energies of biblical speculators were spent on Isaiah instead.

Unlike Isaiah, who seemed to have had ready access to the royal court, Micah's admission to these circles was far more limited. One way this is suggested is by the explicit mention of the name of his humble hometown, Moresheth. "Micah's identification as a Moreshtite implies that he was an outsider to the capitals."[1] Moresheth (Micah 1:1, 14) was situated on a hill about one thousand feet above sea level in the foothills of southwestern Judah, about twenty-five miles southwest of Jerusalem.[2]

Yet even the reference to Moresheth, mentioned nowhere else in the Bible, is insufficient to nudge him away from the gravitational pull of the more luminous Isaiah, around whom he orbits. For we learn that Moresheth was located "in the general proximity of Isaiah's home."[3] It seems poor Micah is destined to forever play backup to headliner Isaiah.

2. Micah's name is related to the content of his prophecy.

In Hebrew, names mean something, and Micah's name is no different. But before we consider what that meaning is, we must note that Micah is actually a shorter form of the name Micaiah. This longer form of the name consists of three elements in Hebrew: Mi (= Who?), ca (= like), and iah (= Yahweh). So, when we supply the verb *is*, we arrive at the meaning "Who is like Yahweh?"—a rhetorical question with the obvious answer of "Nobody!"

This rhetorical question, with which God's people were confronted every time they heard Micah's name, reflects Micah's amazement at a God whose messages of judgment are not his last word to his people. Incredibly, those oracles of woe are repeatedly followed by messages of restoration and forgiveness. Thus, toward the very end of his prophecy, when Micah exclaims, "Who is a God like you, who pardons sin and forgives the transgression of the remnant of his inheritance?" (Micah 7:18), he again expresses his wonder at God's goodness by alluding to the meaning of his own name.

3. Micah prophesied around the same time as several other prophets.

We have already seen that Micah's ministry was far overshadowed by that of Isaiah, his contemporary. Although the precise dates for the ministry of many of the Minor Prophets are difficult to nail down with any precision, tradition maintains that Micah's ministry also overlapped that of at least two other prophets: Hosea and Amos. So, according to tradition, possibly as many as three other biblical prophets who have left books for us in our canon ministered at the same time as Micah. That same tradition asserts, however, that Micah "was a younger contemporary of the other three."[4] It seems, therefore, that our hidden prophet Micah had to deal not only with other practitioners of his craft but also with the fact that he was a junior to them.

There was also a substantial contingent of false prophets with whom Micah had to contend. These prophets directly challenged Micah's message, essentially accusing him and his contemporary true prophets of being liars:

> "Do not prophesy," their [false] prophets say.
> "Do not prophesy about these things;
> disgrace will not overtake us." (2:6)

Then, as now, these self-serving religious figures were led not by the Lord but by their own appetites. The Lord describes them as those who lead his people astray. "They proclaim 'peace' if they have something to eat, but prepare to wage war against anyone who refuses to feed them" (3:5). Against these popular spokespeople, our marginalized and junior prophet was called to speak.

4. In at least one tradition, Micah is mistaken for someone else.

Although extrabiblical traditions regarding Micah are rare, there is one that claims he was a disciple of Elijah![5] Elijah ministered during the reign of Ahab in Israel (874–853). Clearly, this period precedes the time of Micah's ministry by at least a hundred years. So how an assertion that Micah was a disciple of Elijah could possibly be true is interesting to consider.

As we saw above, Micah's name is actually a shorter form of the name Micaiah. And there is indeed a prophet named Micaiah who ministered during the reigns of King Ahab of Israel and King Jehoshaphat of Judah (1 Kings 22:8). Apparently, Jewish tradition has confused our Minor Prophet Micah with this earlier prophet Micaiah son of Imlah[6] even though they clearly ministered at different times.

So not only is poor Micah overshadowed by Isaiah and opposed by false prophets, but he has also been mistaken for someone else. Apparently, this is a hidden prophet whose own life and ministry deserve more concentrated and careful consideration!

5. Micah is more concerned about internal threats to God's people than external threats.

Micah makes it clear that the external threats to God's people are precisely because of the internal threats that they have allowed to go unchecked. The divinely ordained and directed judgments at the hands of Neo-Assyrian kings are outlined in the next section. But Micah lays all of that coming devastation at the feet of the corrupt leaders of Israel and Judah, whose leadership by example has led to a disintegration of moral order throughout the nation.

The religious leaders condone and even encourage pagan cultic practices (Micah 1:5). The wealthy and powerful use their positions of influence and opportunity to deprive the vulnerable of their land, their homes, and their property (2:1–2, 8–9; 7:3). Those in authority manufacture approval for their selfish actions by appointing prophets who are just as ready to indulge their carnal appetites as they are (2:11). The corruption of the legal process and the perversion of moral instruction have left the common people without recourse or direction (3:9–11). The merchants are cheaters, the rich are violent, and everyone lies (6:10–12). With a final, exasperated hyperbole, Micah laments, "The faithful have been swept from the land; not one upright person remains" (7:2). Micah gives voice to the Lord's grief and anguish over what has become of his treasured possession. The uncomfortable similarity of the conditions among the Lord's people during Micah's time to the conditions among the Lord's people today (and every period throughout history) is perhaps one more reason why the church has been content to let the words of Micah languish, virtually hidden as a seldom-visited book within a seldom-read section of Scripture.

6. During Micah's ministry, Israel would cease to exist and Judah would be attacked.

True to his word, God did not allow his people to continue to bring him dishonor on the world stage. He used the dominant world kingdoms to render his judgment against them. At this time in history, the dominant kingdom was the Neo-Assyrian Empire. Early in Micah's ministry, the Neo-Assyrian king, Tiglath-Pileser III (called Pul in the biblical texts), led a campaign to his west that had huge implications for God's people. The northern kingdom of Israel, ruled by Menahem, lost most of its territory to him. Only by paying burdensome tribute to appease the foreign king did Menahem succeed in temporarily staving off complete disaster (2 Kings 15:17–20).

In the annals of Tiglath-Pileser III, which are dated to 738 BC, we have preserved for us his own record of this event. Among the many defeated kings who paid him tribute are found the following:

> I received the tribute of Kuštašpi, the Kummuḫite, Rezin, the Damascene, Menahem, the Samarian.[7]

But this payment bought Israel only a temporary reprieve. The next king of Israel, Pekah, joined forces with Rezin, king of Syria, to oppose Tiglath-Pileser. That proved to be a fatal error in judgment. Tiglath-Pileser's response was swift and deadly. He captured the Syrian capital, Damascus, in 732 BC and substantially reduced the territory of the northern kingdom of Israel. The list of conquered towns and subsequent deportation of their occupants to Assyria is recorded in 2 Kings 15:29. In Tiglath-Pileser's words:

> I carried off [to] Assyria the land of Bīt-Ḫumria (Israel), [… its] "auxiliary [army,"] […] all of its people, […] [I/they killed] Pekah, their king, and I installed Hoshea [as king] over them. I received from them 10 talents of gold, x talents of silver, [with] their [possessions] and [I car]ried them [to Assyria].[8]

Shalmaneser V succeeded Tiglath-Pileser III as king of Assyria, and he was immediately forced to deal with a subversive Hoshea, king of Israel, who had decided to withhold his required tribute. This was the last mistake Israel would make. After a three-year siege against Israel's capital, Samaria, Shalmaneser V captured it in 722 BC and deported the remaining Israelites to Assyria (2 Kings 17:5–6; 18:9–10). The preserved Assyrian accounts of this event are ambiguous with respect to the one to whom credit should be given for the ultimate defeat of Samaria: Shalmaneser V or his successor, Sargon II. The Babylonian Chronicle boasts of Shalmaneser V:

> On 27th Tebet Shalmaneser (V) ascended the throne in Assyria and Babylonia. He shattered Samaria (*šá-ma-ra- '-in*).[9]

But Sargon II takes the credit for himself in his own inscription:

> I besieged and conquered Samarina. I took as booty 27,290 people who lived there. I gathered 50 chariots from them. I taught the rest (of the deportees) their skills. I set my eunuch over them, and I imposed upon them the (same) tribute as the previous king (i.e., Shalmaneser V).[10]

Whether Shalmaneser or Sargon was ultimately responsible, the end was the same. The northern kingdom of Israel ceased to exist from this time onward. The southern kingdom of Judah, spared to this point from experiencing the full brunt of Assyrian power, would also wither in the face of their inescapable presence.

Micah 1:1 states that the last king under whose reign Micah prophesied was Hezekiah. We learn from 2 Kings 18:9 that Shalmaneser's conquest of Samaria, the capital of the ultimately conquered northern kingdom of Israel, began in the fourth year of Hezekiah's reign.

Ten years later, in 701 BC, when Hezekiah revolted against Assyria, another Neo-Assyrian king, Sennacherib, "attacked all the fortified cities of Judah and captured them" (2 Kings 18:13). Among the cities overrun by Sennacherib are those listed in Micah 1:8–15, which include Micah's hometown! The carnage was horrifying. Excavations at one of those cities, Lachish, uncovered "a huge pit into which the Assyrians, presumably, dumped some 1,500 bodies, covering them with pig bones and other rubbish, presumably the Assyrian army's garbage dump."[11] Hezekiah sent Sennacherib a sizable tribute, including "all the silver that was found in the temple of the LORD and in the treasuries of the royal palace" in order to get him to call off his attack (2 Kings 18:14–16), but to no avail.

Sennacherib turned his attention toward Jerusalem, the capital city of Judah, and demanded the full surrender of Hezekiah. Only by a miraculous act were Hezekiah and the much-reduced nation of Judah spared from total annihilation. In 2 Kings 19:35, God sent "the angel of the LORD" to put to death 185,000 Assyrian soldiers. Consequently, Sennacherib slunk back to Nineveh without achieving his desired defeat of Hezekiah. Nevertheless, Sennacherib's own account, as one might imagine, is slightly different. Reading between the lines, we recognize a grudging acknowledgment that he did not actually "conquer" Jerusalem, but that fact is adorned with so many other boasts that it is barely visible:

As for Hezekiah, the Judean, I besieged forty-six of his fortified walled cities and surrounding smaller towns, which were without number. Using packed-down ramps and applying battering rams, infantry attacks by mines, breeches, and siege machines, I conquered (them). I took out 200,150 people, young and old, male and female, horses, mules, donkeys, camels, cattle, and sheep, without number, and counted them as spoil. He himself, I locked up within Jerusalem, his royal city, like a bird in a cage. I surrounded him with earthworks, and made it unthinkable for him to exit by the city gate. His cities which I had despoiled I cut off from his land and gave them to Mitinti, king of Ashdod, Padi, king of Ekron and Ṣilli-bel, king of Gaza, and thus diminished his land. I imposed dues and gifts for my lordship upon him, in addition to the former tribute, their yearly payment.[12]

Micah prophesied in the context of these world-convulsing events. It is not difficult to imagine that, in the face of these enormous challenges, the words of a second-string prophet from a backwater town might have found few listening ears.

7. Micah's prophecy is full of wordplay.

Micah's prophecy is recorded with great literary skill, though this is not always visible in English translations. One stylistic device employed in his writings, hidden in English, is the use of plays on words. For example, some of the towns in Judah overrun by Sennacherib in 701 BC are described in Micah 1:10–15 using words that reflect the meaning of their Hebrew names. It is as though the place-names themselves suggest their ultimate fate. Consider how the meaning of the Hebrew place-names reflects what is prophesied about them:

- "Tell it not in Gath" (1:10).
  "Gath" sounds like the Hebrew word meaning "tell." How ironic that one is not to "tell" something in a town whose name means "tell"!

- "In Beth Ophrah roll in the dust" (1:10).
  "Beth Ophrah" means "house of dust" in Hebrew. Rolling in the dust is a sign of grief, so this would be an appropriate response to the disaster coming upon the country.

- "Pass by naked and in shame, you who live in Shaphir" (1:11).
  "Shaphir" means "beautiful" or "pleasing" in Hebrew. This is another ironic taunt. The inhabitants of a town that was pleasing to view will be depressing to look upon as they are led away naked and in shame as captives to Assyria.

- "Those who live in Zaanan will not come out" (1:11).
  "Zaanan" sounds like the Hebrew word meaning "come out." The residents of this town will also end up doing the opposite of what their town

name means "because, from fear of the enemy, they cower behind their walls."[13]

- "Beth Ezel is in mourning; it no longer protects you" (1:11).
  "Beth Ezel" means "house of taking away" in Hebrew. True to its name, this town will take away any help they could have provided to the failing nation.

- "Those who live in Maroth writhe in pain, waiting for relief" (1:12).
  "Maroth" means "bitterness" in Hebrew. The devastation this town will also experience at the hands of the Assyrians will indeed be bitter.

- "You who live in Lachish, harness fast horses to the chariot" (1:13).
  "Lachish" sounds like the Hebrew term for "fast horses." The people of this town could try in vain to escape their impending doom by the fastest transportation available.

- "Therefore you will give parting gifts to Moresheth Gath" (1:14).
  "Moresheth" sounds like the Hebrew word for "possession." But instead of possessing this town, Judah would have to send it away with

parting gifts as one sends away a bride to a groom.[14] In this case, the very scary groom is Sennacherib!

- "The town of Akzib will prove deceptive" (1:14). "Akzib" means "deception" in Hebrew. Any help expected from this town will indeed be deceptive when it falls ruin to the invading Assyrians.

- "I will bring a conqueror against you who live in Mareshah" (1:15). "Mareshah" sounds like the Hebrew word for conqueror. Here again, the name of the town presages its ultimate fate.

- "The nobles of Israel will flee to Adullam" (1:15). The play on the name Adullam is a little more difficult to discern. It may be related to Semitic roots meaning "to lock in" or "retreat, refuge." If the nobles do, in fact, seek to escape to some refuge in the face of the coming disaster, there they will be imprisoned. Adullam is also the place where David sought to escape from King Saul, who sought his life (1 Samuel 22:1). Now, at the tragic end of the monarchy, the remaining nobles will flee to the same place in a vain attempt to escape Sennacherib, who will seek their lives.

8. Micah presents his case against God's people like a courtroom drama.

Another literary feature found in Micah's prophecy is the use of trial imagery. Presenting his prophecy in this way has the effect of portraying God's people as defendants in a divine lawsuit. God is the plaintiff who uses Micah as his prosecuting attorney against his people. The earth and all its inhabitants comprise the jury. In Micah 1:2, the prophet presents his opening argument:

> Hear, you peoples, all of you,
>> listen, earth and all who live in it,
> that the Sovereign LORD may bear witness against
>> you,
> the Lord from his holy temple.

The defendants, God's people, are badgered with a seemingly endless barrage of questions, evidence, and testimony that leaves no question concerning their guilt:

- "What is Jacob's transgression? Is it not Samaria? What is Judah's high place? Is it not Jerusalem?" (1:5).
- "You descendants of Jacob, should it be said, 'Does the LORD become impatient? Does he do such things?' 'Do not my words do good to the one whose ways are upright? Lately my people have risen up like an enemy. You strip off the

rich robe from those who pass by without a care, like men returning from battle. You drive the women of my people from their pleasant homes. You take away my blessing from their children forever'" (2:7–9).

- "Listen, you leaders of Jacob, you rulers of Israel. Should you not embrace justice, you who hate good and love evil; who tear the skin from my people and the flesh from their bones; who eat my people's flesh, strip off their skin and break their bones in pieces; who chop them up like meat for the pan, like flesh for the pot?" (3:1–3).

- "Hear this, you leaders of Jacob, you rulers of Israel, who despise justice and distort all that is right; who build Zion with bloodshed, and Jerusalem with wickedness. Her leaders judge for a bribe, her priests teach for a price, and her prophets tell fortunes for money. Yet they look for the LORD's support and say, 'Is not the LORD among us? No disaster will come upon us'" (3:9–11).

The prosecution closes its case with God's final instructions to his attorney, Micah:

Stand up, plead my case before the mountains;
let the hills hear what you have to say. (6:1)

Micah then appeals to the jury to give due consideration to the Lord's case, followed by a final outburst from the plaintiff himself to the defendants:

> Hear, you mountains, the LORD's accusation;
>> listen, you everlasting foundations of the
>>> earth.
> For the LORD has a case against his people;
>> he is lodging a charge against Israel.
>
> My people, what have I done to you?
>> How have I burdened you? Answer me.
>>> (6:2–3)

Against Micah's airtight case, God's people have no defense. They are guilty beyond the shadow of a doubt. Consequently, the divine judge hands down their devastating sentence with a series of ominous *therefores*:

- "Therefore I will make Samaria a heap of rubble, a place for planting vineyards. I will pour her stones into the valley and lay bare her foundations" (1:6).
- "Therefore, the LORD says: 'I am planning disaster against this people, from which you cannot save yourselves'" (2:3).
- "Therefore because of you, Zion will be plowed like a field, Jerusalem will become a heap of

rubble, the temple hill a mound overgrown with thickets" (3:12).

- "Therefore, I have begun to destroy you, to ruin you because of your sins" (6:13).
- "Therefore I will give you over to ruin and your people to derision; you will bear the scorn of the nations" (6:16).

That the warranted divine judgment against them should be tempered by any mercy at all is astounding. But it is! In an amazing about-face, the prophet Micah, the attorney for the prosecution, tells us that the plaintiff will pardon sin and forgive transgression. He will not continue to press charges but will have compassion toward the guilty (7:18–19). How justice can possibly be maintained while crimes are dismissed like this will be explored later in this chapter.

9. Micah has his own holiday too!

On the calendar of feasts and fasts for the Greek Orthodox Church, Micah's feast day is January 5 (eve of the Feast of Epiphany) and August 14 (on the Julian calendar, corresponding to January 18 and August 27 on the modern Gregorian calendar).[15] In the book of the anniversaries of the martyrs and other saints commemorated by the Roman Catholic Church, the prophet Micah is remembered on January 15 "in Judea." He shares this feast day with the prophet Habakkuk. According to tradition, the bodies of both of these prophets "were discovered by divine revelation in the days of Theodosius the Elder."[16]

THE GOSPEL ACCORDING TO MICAH

As we have seen, Micah's prophecy includes a scathing indictment of the behavior of God's people in both the northern kingdom of Israel and the southern kingdom of Judah. That behavior included shameless appropriation of the property of the less powerful by whatever means necessary (2:1–2), unrestrained greed (2:8–9), the corruption of justice and abuse of power by government officials (3:1–4), perversion of ecclesiastical offices for personal gain rather than service (3:5–7, 11), and the subordination of morality to personal profit (6:10–12).

This behavior is not describing some random group of misguided miscreants. No, these were God's people! They were the recipients of his care, his protection, his provision, and his guidance. They were supposed to be a shining light on a hill, representing something of the character of God in their interactions with him, with one another, and with outsiders. But their behavior bore no resemblance to God's character at all. Their testimony was false, and they deserved the punishment due anyone who gives false testimony (Deuteronomy 19:18–21). It is no surprise to read that divine judgment would come upon such people.

But unexpectedly, we find intermingled with understandable pronouncements of judgment incomprehensible pronouncements of a future day, on the other side of judgment, when there would be a restoration of a remnant of God's people (2:12–13; 4:1–5:15; 7:11–13). A close reading of these passages reveals that this promised restoration would include far more than a remnant of Israel and Judah. We are told that "many nations" would come to the Lord to learn his ways

(4:2) and that they would live securely, without fear, "for ever and ever" (4:4–5). This will be achieved, we are told, by an eternal, caring shepherd who will ensure their peace and safety (5:2–5).

It is true that some measure of the fulfillment of this prophecy was realized years after the destruction of Israel and Judah when Cyrus, a Persian king, allowed God's people to return to their homeland. But just as the judgment against all human sin was not fully realized by means of the historical judgment of two small nations by foreign empires, so also this promised time of restoration would not be fully realized by the resettlement in the Promised Land of a ragtag group of returning exiles. Something more is being pictured here, something that would only begin to be realized through the coming of Jesus Christ.

Jesus would experience fully the judgment for human ingratitude, injustice, and callousness that Israel and Judah would experience only in part. Jesus's experience of the full measure of divine wrath against sin enables our experience of the restoration Micah foretold that lies on the other side of that wrath. Jesus is the One Micah envisions "whose origins are from of old" (5:2), who accomplishes "our peace" (5:5)—peace with God and peace with one another. When we claim him as our representative in judgment, we can also claim him as our representative in restoration. Quoting from another prophet, Isaiah (the very prophet in whose shadow Micah ministers), the apostle Peter expresses the same truth this way:

> "He himself bore our sins" in his body on the cross,
> so that we might die to sins and live for righteous-
> ness; "by his wounds you have been healed." For

"you were like sheep going astray," but now you have returned to the Shepherd and Overseer of your souls. (1 Peter 2:24–25)

Good news indeed!

WHY MICAH SHOULD MATTER TO YOU

Micah should matter to you only if you are able to recognize in the sinful behavior described by him anything in yourself that looks at all similar. If you do, then trusting in Jesus as your representative in divine judgment delivers you from experiencing that judgment yourself. Justice has been served. Now you are free to enter as fully as you dare into a new kind of life—one in which your fullest human potential is realized. It is the life designed for you by your creator.

Jesus showed us what this life looks like. It is essentially the *opposite* of the life that characterized God's people during the time of Micah's ministry to them. Instead of being focused on personal gain, it is focused on personal sacrifice for others. Instead of using power to exalt oneself, it uses power to serve others. Instead of looking to gods of our own making that we believe can serve us, it emphasizes serving the God who made us. As the apostle Paul reminds us, "And he [Christ] died for all, that those who live should no longer live for themselves but for him who died for them and was raised again" (2 Corinthians 5:15). This new life, therefore, is one that gives a true picture of God to those around us, including those who don't yet know him. When unbelievers see this different way of living as a human being, they will recognize what is missing in their own human experience and will be drawn irresistibly toward it. Because it is, after all, the life for which we were made.

Of course, if we rely on our own strength to live this way, we will likely have as much success doing so as did the people of God in Micah's day. But God has sent the Spirit of Christ to indwell us to give us the ability to live more and more like he did. Living like this will enable us to experience the beginning of the restoration of all things that Micah prophesied. It is beginning now in God's new people, the church, and it will be fully realized when Jesus returns. Thank God that we don't have to wait to begin enjoying it!

DISCUSSION QUESTIONS

1. It was probably surprising to at least some of God's people to hear Micah tell them that God wasn't happy with how they were living. What areas of your own life do you suspect God might not be so happy with?

2. Are you afraid of God's justice? Think about why that might be. Do you think you don't deserve God's mercy? Do you think anyone does? Do you doubt that Jesus has paid the full price for your sin?

3. Some Christians regard their faith as "fire insurance"—that is, it protects them from divine wrath against sin, but it is to be used only in case of an emergency. How might you respond to such Christians after reading the book of Micah? How should we live as believers? Why?

4. What is the strongest motivation for your behavior? That is, why do you do the things you do? Do you fear God's judgment if you don't "behave"? Do you think Jesus's sacrifice covers your sins no matter how you behave? Are you trying to earn points with God? Or are you eager to experience more fully the new life God wants you to enjoy? Do you think about how your life communicates something about God to other people?

5. Have you thought much about how to go about living this new life in Christ? Do you consciously draw on the strength of the Holy Spirit? Or do you try to pull it off on your own?

6. How would you communicate the message of the prophet Micah to someone else?

NAHUM

To say that the road to the biblical region of Nahum is not well traveled would be an extreme understatement. As we approach, we observe that the street signs are rusty and the landscaping is wild and menacing. Those who have visited this biblical hamlet report leaving a bit frightened and even repulsed by its namesake, who seems more than a little mean and vindictive. Indeed, most tourist guides for this portion of the biblical corpus don't even include Nahum on their itineraries. So it is wise for us to exercise due caution as we roll past Nahum's backstreets, boulevards, and alleyways. If we look closely, though, we can discern here and there, under the dust and overgrown with weeds of neglect, evidences of dazzling beauty. As has been true for many geniuses throughout history, the profundity of Nahum has not been appreciated. But the sites we visit during our brief stay in his forgotten book will tug us into a deeper understanding of the gospel itself. We may very well find ourselves providing glowing reviews for other biblical tourists who are considering a visit to this arrestingly powerful book.

LITTLE-KNOWN FACTS ABOUT NAHUM

1. Nahum is mentioned nowhere else in the Bible.

If one performs an electronic search in any Bible software program, or looks in a Bible concordance or the index of a study Bible, no references to the prophet Nahum will be found outside of the book that bears his name. There are also virtually no references to Nahum in the Jewish legends.[1] So we're left with only the few clues provided by Nahum himself to discover any details about this man and his setting.

Immediately in the first verse, we're told that his prophecy concerns Nineveh, the capital of the dreaded Assyrian Empire. Nahum certainly wouldn't be prophesying the fall of Nineveh if it had already happened, so Nahum's prophecy must take place before that event occurred in 612 BC. In 3:8–10, Nahum refers to the fall of the Egyptian city Thebes as having already happened. We know that this event occurred in 663 BC, so we can at least narrow the time of Nahum's prophecy to the period between 663 and 612 BC. That's not very exact—it covers more than a fifty-year period—but it's the best we can do.

One other scrap of information is provided to us in the first verse. We're told that Nahum is an Elkoshite. Unfortunately, we have no idea what this means. It could indicate Nahum was the descendant of a man named Elkosh.[2] Most interpreters, however, believe it means that Nahum came from a place called Elkosh. Where that place is, no one knows. There are no fewer than four possibilities that have been suggested:

- al Kush (also written Alqush or Alqosh), a site fifty miles north of modern Mosul;
- Elkesi, perhaps modern el-Kauzeh;
- Capernaum; and
- a town near Eleutheropolis or Begabar, modern Beit Jibrin.[3]

None of these possible locations for Nahum's hometown has been established with anything approaching certainty.

One last detail of dubious dependability is included here simply because we are desperate at this point for any information about Nahum, however unreliable it may be. According to an ancient manual of iconography known as *Ulpius the Roman*, Nahum was "round-bearded, smoky on the cheeks, with the hairstyle on his forehead like a tall *mu* [that is, shaped like μ or M], a long head, like a man of forty-five, clipped hair."[4] While this description strangely provides us with a lot of information about Nahum's hair, it still leaves significant gaps in our understanding about the man himself.

2. Some argue that Nahum was a false prophet!

Some in the tradition of interpretation have argued Nahum is either a false prophet or at least a "narrow" prophet inferior to the others.[5] These conclusions have been arrived at by some in reaction to the harsh and difficult message that Nahum brings. Nahum has been criticized for allegedly ignoring Israel's own sins and for being overly jubilant at the violent destruction he envisions for the enemies of his people. These scholars have argued that Nahum is more of a zealous patriot who preaches against his nation's enemies than he is a prophet of God. In fact, some draw a parallel between Nahum and false prophets such as Hananiah in Jeremiah 28, whose nationalistic zeal led him to prophesy the destruction of Babylon instead of the divinely ordained subjugation of God's people to Babylon.

Perhaps, it is argued, Nahum's harsh words against Assyria are the result of a similar nationalistic fervor that has eclipsed his proper perception of his true prophetic message—and perhaps even his correct perception of reality! This may be why in some faith communities, the prophet Nahum is "invoked for individuals with mental disorders"![6]

Such conclusions, however, are unwarranted. While Nahum's prophecy is a particularly unrelenting and uncomfortable declaration of judgment against an enemy of God and his people, such indictments are common throughout the prophetic books of the Old Testament. A focused message of judgment should be no more disallowed than a focused message of blessing. Moreover, as we'll see below, while Nahum's prophecy is bad news for Assyria, it is much awaited and welcome good news for God's people, who have repeatedly suffered the cruelty of Assyrian kings.

3. The book of Nahum is in a different place in the Septuagint.

In the Masoretic Text, the Hebrew text on which our English Bibles are based, the book of Nahum follows the book of Micah. But in the Septuagint, the Greek translation of the Old Testament, the book of Nahum follows directly after the book of Jonah. There is a certain logic to this alternative arrangement. Both Jonah and Nahum talk about Nineveh, and their two prophecies complement each other. On the one hand, Jonah demonstrates God's compassion toward the Assyrians. Jonah shows that God is slow to anger, giving the Ninevites the opportunity to repent and avert the divinely appointed disaster headed their way. Nahum, on the other hand, demonstrates God's justice and judgment upon the sinful Assyrians, focused on their capital city, Nineveh. In Nahum, the time for repentance has passed, and it is time for God's sentence upon this nation to be carried out.

Because Jonah and Nahum show these two sides of divine dealings with rebellious human beings, some suggest that these two books form a sort of commentary on Exodus 34:6–7, which describes these same two aspects of God's nature:

> The Lord, the Lord, the compassionate and gracious God, slow to anger, abounding in love and faithfulness, maintaining love to thousands, and forgiving wickedness, rebellion and sin. Yet he does not leave the guilty unpunished.

In fact, Nahum 1:3 obviously alludes to this passage at the very beginning of this prophecy that proclaims that, indeed, in God's dealings with Assyria, the time for not leaving the guilty unpunished has finally arrived.

Both Jonah and Nahum also share an unusual literary feature. They both end with a question, and they are the only books in the Bible to do so! In Jonah's case, the question justifies God's concern for Nineveh. But in Nahum, the final question justifies God's judgment of Nineveh: "All who hear the news about you clap their hands at your fall, for who has not felt your endless cruelty?"

4. Nahum prophesies against Assyria, but his prophecy is for God's people.

In Hebrew, the word Nahum means "comfort." For all the nations that had experienced Assyria's "endless cruelty," it would be comfort indeed to know that the terror of all the earth would finally receive just recompense.

Although horrible enough to contemplate, Nahum 3:1 just skims the surface when it describes Nineveh as "the city of blood, full of lies, full of plunder, never without victims!" The gory details considerately summarized by these short phrases included skinning or dismembering live human beings and displaying the skins or heads of the victims on city walls, trees, or on stakes their friends were made to parade throughout town.[7] Those who thought they could escape this unimaginable horror by securing promises of peace from the Assyrians soon realized the truth of Nahum's description of Nineveh as a city "full of lies."[8] The whole world would breathe a collective sigh of relief to see Assyria disappear from the world stage.[9] The message of Nahum was indeed comfort!

5. Nineveh was destroyed exactly how Nahum prophesied it would be!

Earlier, we considered and rejected the charge of false prophet made against Nahum by some in the history of the interpretation of his prophecy. Further substantiation of Nahum's credentials as a legitimate prophet is provided by the accuracy of his prophecy.

Nahum describes Nineveh's destruction as coming by means of water and fire. In 1:8, Nahum prophesies: "With an overwhelming flood he [God] will make an end of Nineveh." Destructive water is also alluded to in 2:6, which states, "The river gates are thrown open and the palace collapses." Nineveh becomes "like a pool whose water is draining away" (2:8). But fire also appears in the prophecy of Nineveh's destruction. Nahum prophesies that "they will be consumed like dry stubble" (1:10) and their chariots will be consumed by smoke (2:13). In a vision of an already-accomplished future, Nineveh is told "fire has consumed the bars of your gates" (3:13), and consequently, "there the fire will consume you" (3:15).

According to *Lives of the Prophets* 1:3, Nineveh was destroyed when "the lake which surrounds it inundated it during an earthquake, and fire coming from the wilderness burned its higher section." This source is substantiated by other ancient records. A Greek historian by the name of Diodorus Siculus claims that "heavy and continuous rains" resulted in the overflowing of a nearby river that "both inundated a portion of the city and broke down the walls for a distance of twenty stades [e.g., roughly 2.3 miles]."[10] The breached city wall provided easy access for the invading enemy forces.

Nahum's prophecy of Nineveh's destruction by fire and water is supported as well by archaeology. Evidence for flood submergence is provided by "a stratum of pebble and sand ... found a few feet below the surface."[11] Excavations have also shown that "fire was a great instrument in the destruction of the Nineveh palaces." Also found are "calcined alabaster, masses of charred wood and charcoal, [and] colossal statues, slit through with the heat."[12] Thus the end came for Nineveh, by fire and water, just as Nahum had prophesied!

6. The form of Nahum's prophecy adds to its meaning.

The book of Nahum is a literary masterpiece. The prophet employs multiple literary devices, such as simile, metaphor, assonance, repetition, and rhetorical questions, to add power and vividness to his prophecy. Many of these are observable only in the original Hebrew, and a review of all of them would require a book of its own; but we can consider here a few of the more prominent ones.

Already in the first three verses, Nahum sharpens the point of his dire message for Nineveh by his clever use of similar-sounding words. That God has determined to avenge his oppressed people is underscored by the machine gun repetition of the Hebrew root *n-q-m*, which has the basic meaning of "to avenge" or "to take vengeance": "The LORD is a jealous and *avenging* God; the LORD *takes vengeance* and is filled with wrath. The LORD *takes vengeance* on his foes and vents his wrath against his enemies" (Nahum 1:2). To further highlight this triple trouble, Nahum surrounds this verse with words that sound similar to *n-q-m*. In 1:1, we are reminded of *n-q-m* by the sound of Nahum's name, *naḥûm*. In 1:3, we are reminded of *n-q-m* by a double use of the word translated as "leave unpunished," *n-q-h*. Consequently, one cannot read the first three verses of Nahum without a clear understanding of what this prophecy is all about.

Another literary feature that Nahum employs is his use of language to paint a picture. This draws the reader into the scene. It is as though we are bystanders who are present as the prophetic fulfillment unfolds before us. This literary device is most observable in 3:2–3. These verses portray the chaos of battle. Adrenaline levels are high. The enemy is all around. It is unclear who is friend and who is foe. Nahum puts us right there in the desperate struggle, panicked confusion, and disorientation of hand-to-hand combat. The terse Hebrew phrases employed present the reader with rapid-fire snapshots of the melee. The English translation accurately conveys the sensory overload achieved by this literary tour de force:

> The crack of whips,
>> the clatter of wheels,
> galloping horses
>> and jolting chariots!
> Charging cavalry,
>> flashing swords
>> and glittering spears!
> Many casualties,
>> piles of dead,
> bodies without number,
>> people stumbling over the corpses.

The strikingly effective vividness of this verbally portrayed mayhem compels the reader to flee to the "refuge in times of trouble" (1:7).

One final literary feature of Nahum that we may consider is his use of a "broken acrostic." An acrostic is a composition in which each line begins with a successive letter of the alphabet. A clear biblical example of this is the description of "the wife of noble character" in Proverbs 31:10–31. The first verse (31:10) begins with the first letter of the Hebrew alphabet, and each subsequent verse begins with the next letter right up to the final verse, which starts with the last letter of the Hebrew alphabet. Nahum 1:2–10 is sometimes called a "broken acrostic" because these verses do not begin with all the letters of the Hebrew alphabet, and also because the order of the Hebrew letters with which these verses do begin is not precisely alphabetical. While these facts have led some to argue against the presence of an acrostic at all,[13] others have submitted that the very "brokenness" of this acrostic is a literary device intentionally employed by Nahum. Scholar Tremper Longman III, for example, argues:

> It is possible to … suggest a connection between the content of the poem and the sense of chaos imparted by the broken acrostic…. The appearance of the Divine Warrior is accompanied by massive cosmic upheaval. Creation order turns to cosmic disorder. The partial acrostic is a poetic device for communicating the message that God, the Warrior who melts mountains and dries up seas, is present.[14]

Another possible function of the broken acrostic is to communicate textually the brokenness that Nahum is prophesying against Nineveh. Its palace will collapse (2:6); it will be pillaged, plundered, and stripped bare (2:10). Just as Nineveh will be broken, therefore, so the acrostic used to describe it is broken. In form as well as content, the message of Nineveh's demise is inescapably clear.

7. The church has been historically uncomfortable with Nahum's prophecy.

A lectionary is "a collection of readings or selections from the Scriptures, arranged and intended for proclamation during the worship of the People of God." The use of lectionaries is attested already in the fourth century and has continued down through the history of the Christian church.[15] Lectionaries are a way to ensure that all parts of God's Word are regularly visited by the church in the course of its regular worship over a period of one to three years. It is surprising to see, therefore, that in most historical and contemporary lectionaries no readings from the book of Nahum occur. One can only conclude that the subject matter of Nahum and its unsettling mode of presentation have led many to judge it unsuitable for worship settings. Indeed, without a fuller understanding of the prophecy's place and function in the larger setting of redemptive history, anyone would be uncomfortable with isolated readings from the book. Can you imagine, for example, the following framed, cross-stitched verses hanging prominently in a believer's home?

"I am against you," declares the LORD Almighty.
    "I will lift your skirts over your face.
I will show the nations your nakedness
    and the kingdoms your shame.
I will pelt you with filth,
    I will treat you with contempt
    and make you a spectacle." (Nahum 3:5–6)

It would be enough to send visitors running for the door!

8. Nahum has his own holiday too!

The prophet Nahum is remembered on December 1 in the calendar of feasts and fasts for the Greek Orthodox Church, and in the book of the anniversaries of the martyrs and other saints commemorated by the Roman Catholic Church (on the Julian calendar, corresponding to December 14 on the modern Gregorian calendar).[16]

9. Nahum's tomb may be in jeopardy.

In the town of al Kush (or Alqosh)—which may be the hometown of Nahum (see above)—is a tomb that many believe is his. This tomb of potentially such great historical significance is, however, in danger from both internal factors and external factors. The Jewish Press has recently reported that:

> According to local news reports, Nahum's tomb has
> been deteriorating and is in danger of collapsing. The

town of Alqosh has been protected by Peshmerga forces since ISIS overran the Iraqi army in the region.[17]

THE GOSPEL ACCORDING TO NAHUM

Another literary feature of Nahum's prophecy we have yet to discuss helps us understand more deeply the judgment he prophesies against Nineveh, Assyria's glorious but doomed capital city, and also an alternative to that judgment. This feature consists of a single Hebrew word that appears in just two places—but critical places—in the book: near the beginning and near the end. By placing this single word at these critical places, Nahum signals to the reader the central point of the entire book. This central point has everything to do with the meaning of this Hebrew word. The word is *'ābar*, and its basic meaning is "to pass over." In English translations, however, the presence of this Hebrew word at these two critical places is often not seen because it is usually rendered in more contextually nuanced ways. Its presence is indicated below by the italicized words in the two verses in which it occurs.

> 1:8—"But with an *overwhelming* flood he will make an end of Nineveh; he will pursue his foes into the realm of darkness."
> 3:19—"Nothing can heal you; your wound is fatal. All who hear the news about you clap their hands at your fall, for who has not felt your *endless* cruelty?"

In Nahum 1:8, the prophet uses the Hebrew word *'ābar* to describe the floodwaters—both literal and figurative—that would overwhelm or "pass over" Nineveh and bring it to an end. In Nahum 3:19, the prophet again uses the Hebrew word *'ābar*. But this time, he uses it to describe the cruelty of the Assyrians. It was "endless" in the sense that it had "passed over" every nation they had encountered without any decrease in severity.

By using the same word in a description of Assyria's cruelty and in a description of God's judgment of Assyria, Nahum shows how God's judgment fits the crime. But God's judgment was not inevitable, of course. In the verse just before the judgment described in 1:8, we're told, "The LORD is good, a refuge in times of trouble. He cares for those who trust in him" (1:7). Indeed, in the writings of the earlier prophet Jonah, we saw the Ninevites choose this refuge from prophesied divine judgment and then have that judgment averted. In their earlier time of repentance, they had experienced God's mercy when his judgment passed them by.

So there are two possible options with respect to God's judgment. It can "pass over" the guilty, in the sense of their full experience of it, or it can "pass over" them, in the sense of their exemption from it. We see both of these options represented in Exodus 12:23, where Moses describes how the Egyptians will experience the coming divine wrath differently than will the Israelites: "When the LORD goes through [*'ābar*] the land to strike down the Egyptians, he will see the blood on the top and sides of the doorframe and will pass over [*pāsaḥ*] that doorway, and he will not permit the destroyer to enter your houses and strike you down." You probably noticed that a synonym was used for *'ābar* in the second half of the verse. This word, *pāsaḥ*, is used in the Bible to refer to the Passover, associated with the lamb whose blood was placed on the doorframes of the Israelite homes. This blood averted the divine wrath, causing it to pass by those whose trust was in the Lord.

The ultimate fulfillment of the Passover lamb is realized in Jesus Christ, the Lamb of God. It is his blood that averts divine wrath for those who claim him as their Lord. Jesus came to have God's judgment *pass over* him, in the sense of fully experiencing it, so that God's judgment would *pass over* all who believe in Jesus, in the sense of being exempted from it. Because, as Nahum reminds us, God "cares for those who trust in him" (1:7). So the bad news is that all of us, like the Assyrians, deserve God's wrath (Romans 3:10–19). But the good news, or gospel, is that Jesus has already experienced that wrath for those who believe in him (Romans 5:9).

WHY NAHUM SHOULD MATTER TO YOU

The book of Nahum can understandably make us uncomfortable. We don't like to hear about judgment, and Nahum proclaims almost uninterrupted judgment! But we can't appreciate the full impact of Nahum's message until we realize that the judgment he relentlessly describes is that which we also deserve.

As we read Nahum, we can eventually be lured into adding our "Amen!" to the judgment decreed for such a wicked people. But then we remember that all of us at one time were like the people of Nineveh—enemies of God and deserving his wrath (Ephesians 2:3). And reading about the divine judgment that will surely come against such enemies of God enables us to understand and appreciate more fully what Jesus has delivered us from. After all, who needs to be delivered if there is nothing to be delivered from? We not only realize what we've been delivered from, but we also see what Jesus was *not* delivered from. God's judgment against his enemies is just, and Jesus—the only One who deserved to have it "pass over" or bypass him—was willing to have the incomprehensible enormity of it fully "pass over" or rain down upon him. What we deserved, he experienced. What he deserved, we experience. We are given access into the refuge of God's love and care. We no longer have to fear God's judgment.

But when we trust in the Lord, we are still subject to mistreatment by those who oppose God and his people. How should we deal with these modern-day "Assyrians," those who marginalize, oppress, and murder God's people? The biblical answer directs our focus in two directions—one on ourselves and one on our enemies.

Regarding ourselves, the New Testament echoes the reassurance provided by the book of Nahum: There will be a day when we will be delivered from the presence and power of sin, just as we have already been delivered from the penalty of sin. "There will be no more death or mourning or crying or pain" (Revelation 21:4), because those who cause it will be removed. Several hundred years after Nahum, the apostle Paul encourages similarly beleaguered believers with a related message: "God is just: He will pay back trouble to those who trouble you and give relief to you who are troubled … This will happen when the Lord Jesus is revealed from heaven in blazing fire with his powerful angels" (2 Thessalonians 1:6–7).

A second biblical answer to the question of how we should deal with contemporary "Assyrians" is even more profound. It directs our attention not to ourselves and our situation but to our oppressors and their situation. Perhaps disappointingly for us, God does not direct us to strike back at them. But he does direct us to participate with him in retaliatory redemption. In one sense, we are to continue to pray for their destruction. It is all right for us to pray for them to cease to exist! But our prayer should be that they cease to exist by becoming new creations through faith in Jesus Christ (2 Corinthians 5:17). God miraculously transformed us from being his enemies to being his friends. Now he calls on us to participate in his redemptive program by our words and actions, empowered by the Holy Spirit, to eliminate a few more of his enemies in the same way. We have fled to the refuge God has provided in Jesus. Let's do what we can, by his power, to let other people know that the door is still open to this refuge from the overwhelming flood of God's judgment that is certainly coming.

DISCUSSION QUESTIONS

1. After reading Nahum's prophecy against Nineveh, what would you say are the reasons for God's message of judgment against them? Do you recognize any of these things in your own life?

2. What are the opposites of Nineveh's sins? Do you recognize any of these things in your own life? What could you do to make them more characteristic of your life?

3. Is it right to look forward to the judgment of the enemies of God and his people? How does the focus of redemptive history on Jesus Christ affect how we should view this judgment?

4. Have you ever been impatient with the timing of God's judgment? Have you ever taken vengeance into your own hands? Have you ever been tempted to?

5. Which would you rather see: the judgment of those who oppress God's people or their conversion to faith in Jesus Christ?

6. How would *you* fare if God's judgment against people were to come as swiftly and unmercifully as you would like it to?

HABAKKUK

Escaping the harsh environs of Nahum, we immediately find ourselves in the neighboring region of Habakkuk. Guidebooks for this area don't provide much for us, so we decide to seek some direction from the locals. We pull off the highway and enter a roadside chapel, where we find Habakkuk himself deeply engaged in prayer. Because the space is small, and because Habakkuk is quite passionate in his vocal prayer, we cannot help overhearing. He is obviously upset about something and is seeking some answers from God. Habakkuk seems aware of our presence during this sacred dialogue, but he continues laying bare his heart without moderation. One is forced to conclude that Habakkuk *wants* us to overhear his prayer. It seems as though he wants us to identify with and share his concerns so that his prayer becomes our own. We take a seat and listen in. It doesn't take us long to recognize in his words struggles that resonate with us. We find ourselves just as curious as Habakkuk is about how God will address them.

LITTLE-KNOWN FACTS ABOUT HABAKKUK

1. Almost everything about Habakkuk is a mystery—even the meaning of his name!

Almost every personal detail about this hidden prophet remains well and truly hidden. The biblical text does not even provide a narrative describing Habakkuk's call to be a prophet. His book simply begins with a bare description of Habakkuk as "the prophet" (1:1).

The biblical text also provides no indication of Habakkuk's lineage, but the pseudepigraphical *Lives of the Prophets* (12:1) records that he "was of the tribe of Simeon, from the countryside of Bethzouchar."[1] Additional extrabiblical information is found in a fascinating Jewish tradition that identifies Habakkuk's mother as the well-to-do woman in Shunem, whose son Elisha restored to life (2 Kings 4:8).[2] This identification is buttressed by the derivation of Habakkuk's name from the word translated "hold" in Elisha's words to the Shunammite woman in 2 Kings 4:16: "About this time next year … you will hold a son in your arms." This traditional derivation stems from the similarity of the Hebrew word for "hold" (*ḥōbeqet*) with the Hebrew word for "Habakkuk" (*ḥăbaqqûq*).[3] Though this is an interesting similarity, it is only a superficial one. Even an untrained linguist can see that Habakkuk's name contains a couple more *q*'s than the word for "hold." Furthermore, because the ministry of Elisha is usually dated to sometime between 850 and 800 BC,[4] this identification of Habakkuk's mother as the Shunammite woman of 2 Kings 4 requires Habakkuk to have lived far earlier than the period during which he is believed to have ministered.

We must acknowledge, though, that the book of Habakkuk contains no specific historical reference by means of which we may confidently date his ministry. Nevertheless, based on the situation Habakkuk describes in 1:6–11, we can speculate with a fair degree of probability concerning the time of his ministry. These verses suggest Habakkuk lived and ministered during the rise of the Neo-Babylonian Empire (626–539 BC), referred to simply in 1:6 as "the Babylonians"—a people group who had entered Babylonia between 1000 and 900 BC and eventually extended their control over the entire region. We can perhaps narrow the period of Habakkuk's ministry even further based on the societal dysfunction he describes in 1:2–4. This would have to be a time when the social and moral reform imposed by King Josiah (640–609 BC) had lost its hold over the populace. And clearly Habakkuk is concerned about an impending Babylonian invasion, one that Judah would begin to experience in 605 after Nebuchadnezzar's victory at Carchemish. It seems most likely, therefore, that Habakkuk ministered at some time between 609 and 605 BC, or soon afterward.

While we have already discounted a connection between the meaning of Habakkuk's name and the Hebrew word meaning "hold," the meaning of Habakkuk's name remains an enigma. It does not appear to have a Hebrew origin. It seems, rather, to be derived from Akkadian and refer, oddly, to a garden plant.[5] What prompted Habakkuk's parents to give their son such a name is anyone's guess. Perhaps it was no more unusual than naming a baby Rose or Myrtle.

History provides us with at least two suggestions regarding Habakkuk's appearance. One is provided by Donatello, who sculpted it in marble between 1427 and 1436. Titled *Lo Zuccone*, the sculpture is believed to be a rendering of the prophet Habakkuk. *Zuccone* means "pumpkin," usually understood to refer to the bald head of the figure. This sculpture is supposed to have been the artist's favorite, and it remains in Florence today.[6] Contrasting with this image of baldness is a description provided in *Ulpius the Roman* that describes Habakkuk as "round-bearded, not fully clipped hair, with the hairstyle on his forehead like a *mu* [that is, μ or M], [and] both his head and beard sprinkled with gray hairs."[7] Unfortunately, both of these depictions are simply guesses, with the contrast between them only highlighting the fact that Habakkuk's true appearance is lost to history.

2. The book of Habakkuk contains no message explicitly directed toward God's people!

Unlike most other prophetic books, the book of Habakkuk contains no message explicitly directed to God's people—or any other people for that matter! Instead, we are invited to listen in on Habakkuk's complaints to God as well as to God's answers to those complaints. Because the issues Habakkuk boldly places before God are issues that every believer faces, we are irresistibly drawn in to the dialogue. What Habakkuk finally ends up learning under divine tutelage, we also learn. And it is in that way that Habakkuk catches us up into a learning moment, perhaps even without our being aware.

At times, however, Habakkuk's words can be a bit unsettling to Christians unaccustomed to speaking with God so frankly. Indeed, Jewish tradition judges that, just as other "pious" men such as Moses, David, and Jeremiah occasionally did when "carried away by their prayers," Habakkuk "addressed unbecoming words to God."[8] But Habakkuk's honesty reminds God's people that we also can be honest with God about our struggles as well as our joys.

3. Habakkuk might have been a musician or worship leader in the temple.

Evidence that Habakkuk may have had some formal position as a leader of worship in the temple is drawn from a variety of sources. One of those sources is the book of Habakkuk itself. In chapter 3, we find the word "Selah" used three times (3:3, 9, 13). While the precise meaning of this word is uncertain, it seems to be a technical term that indicates the style of music or some sort of direction regarding its performance.[9] Another technical term, *shigionoth*, is found in 3:1. Unfortunately, our understanding of the meaning of this word is also unclear, but it too may refer to the style of the composition or the manner of its performance.[10] We are on far more solid ground when we examine the last part of 3:19, where we are provided with clear musical direction: "For the director of music. On my stringed instruments." It is unclear, however, whether this suggests that Habakkuk himself directed the music or that he composed this piece for someone else to perform.

That Habakkuk himself was a worship leader (that is, a Levite) finds support, however meager, from the first line of the Greek version of the apocryphal composition entitled "Bel and the Dragon." In it, we find Habakkuk referred to as "the son of Jesus of the tribe of Levi."[11] This Levitical identification is also strengthened, according to some interpreters, by the use of the quasi-technical word "watch" in 2:1 ("I will stand at my watch")—a term used in other places to refer to the Levitical "watches" of service at the temple, often particularly associated with music.[12]

This layering of suggestions from the text itself, hints from tradition, and the possible use of a technical word led at least one commentator to conclude, "Habakkuk was probably an official temple musician-prophet."[13] Of course, the tradition of Habakkuk's Levitical lineage is at odds with the tradition observed above that states he is a descendant of Simeon. Nevertheless, it seems incontrovertible that at least the last chapter of Habakkuk's prophecy finds its setting in the formal worship of the community. This leads to the question of whether that last chapter was indeed written by Habakkuk.

4. There is some question whether the last chapter was written by Habakkuk.

One of the original seven Dead Sea Scrolls found in Qumran Cave 1 in 1947 (1QpHab) was a pesher on the book of Habakkuk. *Pesher* means "interpretation" in Hebrew, so a pesher is an ancient Jewish commentary or interpretation of Scripture. Interestingly, this pesher on the book of Habakkuk, which dates from the first century before Christ, comments only on the first two chapters—the psalm of chapter 3 is absent! Does this mean that the copy of Habakkuk on which the pesher, or commentary, is based did not include chapter 3? Is the copy of the pesher we have found incomplete? We simply do not know.[14]

The fact that the pesher on Habakkuk does not include chapter 3 has led many biblical scholars to conclude that chapter 3 is not an original part of the book. Rather, they propose, the chapter was added either much later in the postexilic period or was indeed an ancient composition, even predating Habakkuk, that was subsequently appended to his prophecy in the exilic period.[15]

Arguing, however, for Habakkuk's authorship of this chapter is the continuity of theme throughout the entire book and the pivotal role this powerful conclusion plays for the entire composition. There is also strong manuscript evidence for the inclusion of chapter 3 in the book.[16] Consequently, there does not seem to be any compelling reason to reject Habakkuk's authorship of this chapter of the book that has been handed down to us.

5. In extrabiblical writings and early Christian art, Habakkuk is associated with the prophet Daniel and with Christ.

In the apocryphal composition "Bel and the Dragon" referenced above, we are told how an angel tells Habakkuk to bring a meal to the prophet Daniel, who is in exile in Babylon. The angel lifts and carries Habakkuk by his hair (!) from Judea all the way to Babylon, where the angel sets him down to give the meal to Daniel, who at that time was in the lions' den. After Habakkuk delivers the meal, the angel promptly returns him to Judea—about five hundred miles away (15:33–39).[17]

The pseudepigraphical composition *Lives of the Prophets* also recounts this story, providing additional details. In this account, we learn that Habakkuk's regular practice of distributing food is miraculously extended to Daniel in faraway Babylon: "He [that is, Habakkuk] was living in his own district and ministering to those who were harvesting his field. When he took the food, he prophesied to his own family, saying, 'I am going to a far country, and I will come quickly. But if I delay, take [food] to the harvesters.' And when he had gone to Babylon and given the meal to Daniel, he approached the harvesters as they were eating and told no one what had happened" (12:4–7).[18]

This story led to Habakkuk being frequently pictured with Daniel in church art. For example, in the reliefs of the famous door panels of Saint Sabina on the Aventine Hill in Rome is a carved depiction of this scene. It is the only nonbiblical scene among all the others depicted there. This event, therefore, held a high degree of significance or fascination at least among believers in the early fifth century AD when it was carved.[19]

Habakkuk was also associated with Christ himself! One common way this connection is made is based on the Greek translation of the Hebrew text of the last part of Habakkuk 3:2. Woodenly, the Hebrew text may be translated as "In the midst of years make known." But the word "years" in Hebrew is identical to the word for the number "two." So, another translation possibility, however unlikely from the context, would be "In the midst of two make known." The Septuagint, the Greek translation of the Old Testament, renders this "In the midst of two creatures you will be made known."

This is subsequently understood by later Christian artists and interpreters of the Greek text to be a reference to the ox and ass that were present at Jesus's birth. Thus, Habakkuk comes to be associated with the incarnation of Christ.[20]

Before leaving this consideration of Habakkuk in Christian art, we must pause to consider the inscription on a seventh-century mosaic in the apse of the Church of Hosios David in Thessaloniki, Greece. The mosaic depicts Ezekiel and Habakkuk standing under Jesus. The inscription on the mosaic tells of how the daughter of the Emperor Maximus had secretly become a Christian and had subsequently asked her father for a bathhouse, which she converted into a church while he was away. She also commissioned a painter to produce a picture of the Virgin Mary in the eastern apse of the church. Nearly finished with the painting, the artist returned to work one day and found that the Virgin had transformed into Christ, seated on a cloud, with the prophets Ezekiel and Habakkuk on either side, looking amazed. Maximus, upon finding out about the church, put his daughter to death and burned the church. The image, however, survived, and a monastery was built on the site in the ninth century.[21] Whether or not this tale is true, it does provide further evidence of the importance of Habakkuk in the historical church's visual expression of its faith.

6. Habakkuk 2:4 was pivotal in the conversion of Martin Luther.

When the apostle Paul wrote to the believers in Rome, near the beginning of his letter he told them that he was not ashamed of the gospel because "it is the power of God that brings salvation to everyone who believes" (1:16). Paul goes on in the next verse to assert that the "righteousness of God" is revealed in the gospel and that righteousness "is by faith from first to last, just as it is written: 'The righteous will live by faith.'" Paul is quoting here from Habakkuk 2:4, and it is this verse over which Martin Luther spent many hours of study and contemplation as he sought to understand the gospel of grace.

Initially, Luther understood "the righteousness of God" as referring to God's standard of righteousness, which he was all too aware that he failed to meet. Contrary to providing him comfort or "good news," this "righteousness of God" was a painful reminder to him of the judgment that his sin deserved. However, after going back again and again to this passage, it began to dawn on Luther that he had been reading Paul incorrectly. Luther realized that he had been so focused on his negative understanding of the "righteousness of God" that he had neglected the rest of verse 17, where Paul cited Habakkuk 2:4. The "righteousness of God," Luther realized, is not an impossible requirement of the believer but rather a divine gift to the believer by means of faith. And this faith-transmitted divine righteousness means life for the believer!

It is Luther's revised understanding of Habakkuk 2:4 that enabled him to turn the corner from spiritual despair to exuberant joy. In his words, "Here I felt that I was altogether born again and had entered paradise itself."[22] The prophet Habakkuk was used by God, therefore, not only to provide comfort to the people of Judah in the midst of trials from inside and outside their kingdom but also to enliven the heart of a Reformer who would take God's message of justification by grace through faith to the entire world!

7. Habakkuk has his own holiday too!

It is interesting to note, in light of Habakkuk's association with Christ in early Christian art, that Habakkuk is celebrated in the vicinity of Christmas. On the calendar of feasts and fasts for the Greek Orthodox Church, Habakkuk's feast day is December 2 (on the Julian calendar, corresponding to December 15 on the modern Gregorian calendar).[23] In the book of the anniversaries of the martyrs and other saints commemorated by the Roman Catholic Church, the prophet Habakkuk is remembered on January 15 "in Judea." He shares this feast day with the prophet Micah. According to tradition, the bodies of both of these prophets "were discovered by divine revelation in the days of Theodosius the Elder."[24]

THE GOSPEL ACCORDING TO HABAKKUK

If ever there was an urgent call for good news in the midst of personal angst and theological short-circuiting, Habakkuk provides us with one. He cries out in anguish over the injustices and cruelties that people—God's people!—are perpetrating all around him. One would expect this kind of behavior from those who reject God, but not from those who have been separated out from the rest of humanity for God's special care and guidance. Even though he doesn't have to give an account of himself to human beings, God graciously answers Habakkuk's complaint; but what an answer! Habakkuk learns that God will certainly judge the unjust and wicked. But God shocks Habakkuk by telling him that he will use the unjust and wicked Babylonians to do it! This leads Habakkuk to cry out to God in profound theological frustration: "Why are you silent while the wicked swallow up those more righteous than themselves?" (Habakkuk 1:13). God mercifully lets Habakkuk in on his divine plan. God will judge the Babylonians also, but in his own timing, not Habakkuk's. Having had his perspective gently realigned by God himself, the prophet summarizes his learning in the beautiful last chapter—a chapter that communicates good news in the very midst of his trials. Habakkuk comes to realize that his only true comfort—physically and theologically—cannot be found in his own understanding, in the behavior of his countrymen that he approves, or even in circumstances that turn out the way or in the manner he would like. No, the only true source of ultimate comfort and confidence can be found exclusively in the One who can never fail, change, or disappoint—the Sovereign Lord himself (3:17–19).

This is precisely the gospel that, centuries later, Jesus himself communicated to his people when they were once again troubled, frustrated, and victimized by the injustices and cruelty of others. Like Habakkuk, God's people under Roman rule had to be reminded not to look to their circumstances for comfort and contentment, because those circumstances can change in a heartbeat. Instead, they should find their security, their direction, their purpose, and their comfort in their all-powerful, all-compassionate, all-knowing God. This is good news because it means a comfort and contentment that is as enduring as the One who guarantees it.

It is certainly true, however, for later believers as for Habakkuk, that how God accomplishes his divine purposes often involves circumstances and situations that are entirely the opposite of what his people prefer. Jesus doesn't sugarcoat this reality; instead, he immediately redirects our attention, as God did for Habakkuk, to the One who embodies the resolution of that difficult reality: "In this world you will have trouble. But take heart! I have overcome the world" (John 16:33).

In words that complement Habakkuk 3:17–19, Jesus invites us also to find that reassuring comfort and rest in him: "Come to me, all you who are weary and burdened, and I will give you rest" (Matthew 11:28). He is the Good Shepherd who leads everyone who trusts in him beside still waters—even though the waters might very well be flowing in the presence of our enemies (Psalm 23:5)! The good news is not that we'll avoid trouble the rest of our days. Rather, the good news is that our strength and encouragement are found in the One who has ultimately overcome those troubles.

WHY HABAKKUK SHOULD MATTER TO YOU

The message of Habakkuk should matter to us because we can readily identify with his problem and need to readily identify with the solution he realized. Like Habakkuk, we may get confused or discouraged when circumstances head south, maybe even to the deep south! We may have been wrongly advised by ear-tickling salesmen for a pseudo-Christianity that professing our faith in Jesus should lead to a fairy-tale life of rainbows and unicorns. When we unexpectedly experience hardship of one sort or another, we may feel like our theological wires have been crossed. Bad things are supposed to happen to bad people and good things to good people, right? But Habakkuk's dialogue with God reminds us that such thinking reveals a life focus that is out of alignment. It reveals to us where we are really looking for our confidence and strength. Hard times can show us when we're looking in the wrong places for those things.

In the swirl of troubles that can descend upon us as quickly and as violently as a tornado, we can be tempted to look for security and comfort in those things that we can see and over which we believe we have some control. But the things we can see pass away. And the control we believe we have over any situation isn't real. In the midst of turmoil, we, like Habakkuk, may need to reorient our thoughts. We need to remember that God is in control and that he has never failed his people in the past. And unlike the illusory things we may turn to in crises, the security and comfort God provides is more inner than outer, more foundational than superficial, and more enduring than ephemeral. Jesus has secured our relationship with God so strongly that nothing can snatch us out of his hand (John 10:29), no matter how troubling or tragic the situation may be. There is nothing that could matter more than that truth in the midst of a life-shaking experience.

Habakkuk was encouraged to have patient hope, patient trust, and patient confidence in God—and in nothing else. In addition to reminding us of our only true rock in a storm, Habakkuk also reminds us that, in the very midst of that storm, we need to bring our concern to the only One who can do something about it. Similarly, the apostle Peter tells the church, "Cast all your anxiety on him because he cares for you" (1 Peter 5:7). We see from Habakkuk's own struggles, however, that the thing God changes may not be the circumstances that trouble us but our own understanding of where our true security lies as those circumstances unfold. In any trouble, we may find comfort in God and in his care for us. Our circumstances may change, but God's care for us never will. Our future is secure. God's authority over death and all the damaging and discouraging effects of sin has been proven by Jesus's resurrection from the dead. We now have a "living hope" of an inheritance that God will certainly bring about (1 Peter 1:3–5). Now that's something we can take comfort in!

Nevertheless, like Habakkuk, it is easy for us to lose focus at times. Things are going to happen that we don't understand. Some things we are trusting in will prove unworthy of that trust. And God will occasionally push us, as he did Habakkuk, out of our comfort zones so that we remember where our true comfort and security lie. When we redirect our focus toward our always reliable, always faithful, and all-powerful God, then we will be able to say along with Habakkuk, "Though [all sorts of horrible things may happen], yet I will rejoice in the LORD, I will be joyful in God my Savior. The Sovereign LORD is my strength; he makes my feet like the feet of a deer, he enables me to tread on the heights" (Habakkuk 3:17–19). The depths of the catastrophe may remain, but we'll be able to view them from the heights because we draw our strength from God's unlimited resources.

DISCUSSION QUESTIONS

1. When things go wrong, what is typically your immediate reaction? Do you curse your situation? Does your reaction reveal a misaligned focus? What is the ultimate source of peace and comfort in your life?

2. Where do you run when your world has turned upside down? Do you run to something that will help you forget? Do you simply shut down? Do you believe you can find peace and comfort by turning to God? What has God done for his people, and for you, in the past? Does God change? Have you changed?

3. Turning to God for strength in trials sounds nice, but what does it mean? What practical things could this include? What are the things Habakkuk did? How could your community of faith help you with this?

4. In Habakkuk 3:17, the prophet lists several things that he might be tempted to trust in instead of God. What things are you particularly susceptible to trusting in instead of God?

5. Habakkuk had a problem with the way God was going to deal with the sin of his people. If Habakkuk were in control, he probably would have chosen another way. Are you confident that how God is dealing with issues in your own life is the best way? If not, are you able to be as honest with God about it as Habakkuk was?

6. What was your last "Habakkuk moment"—when you became aware that you had been trusting in the wrong things? How did God bring you to an awareness of that?

ZEPHANIAH

Having had our faith refreshed at the biblical rest area of Habakkuk, we merge back onto the theological thoroughfare that snakes its way through the hidden prophets. Traffic is unsurprisingly light as we wend our way toward the prophet Zephaniah. He is difficult to locate, and when we do find him, we soon realize that we're navigating through a more upscale neighborhood. Zephaniah is not one whose upbringing would lead us to believe that he would readily mingle with the common people. His work would seem more naturally undertaken in boardrooms, halls of government, and in the august gatherings of religious leaders. But we learn that Zephaniah's speech has alienated him from precisely those privileged classes that might have expected something better from him. And he doesn't just gently scold; he lambastes. He radically departs from the acceptable rhetorical style that instructs one to start a critique by pointing out the encouraging, positive points before moving on to the more uncomfortable, negative notes. Zephaniah begins instead with a judgment oracle more powerful than that delivered by almost any of his prophetic colleagues. Encouragement does come, but only after Zephaniah has completed his devastating opening remarks.

LITTLE-KNOWN FACTS ABOUT ZEPHANIAH

1. Zephaniah was probably related to royalty!

The first verse of Zephaniah's prophecy identifies him as the great-great-grandson of Hezekiah. There are good reasons to believe that this Hezekiah is none other than King Hezekiah, who "did what was right in the eyes of the LORD" (2 Kings 18:3).[1] Zephaniah would not need to further clarify that his ancestor Hezekiah was indeed the king if Zephaniah's contemporaries already knew this. In fact, to point it out might seem to be pushing his royal ancestry a bit too hard. The reference to King Hezekiah, however, during the reign of King Josiah (640–609 BC), who was carrying out similar national reform, would give Zephaniah's words even greater force. King Josiah was himself the great-grandson of Hezekiah, so he and Zephaniah were probably distant cousins.

That Zephaniah was descended from royalty and a cousin of the reigning king would also explain why he "concerns himself only with the upper echelons of society—princes, judges, prophets, priests (1:8–9; 3:3–4)—and not directly with the average Israelite."[2] Zephaniah's credentials would have given him access to the elite of his day, when Assyria's glory days were behind her and the Babylonians were not yet an immediate threat. It was a time when the officials of Judah perhaps entertained thoughts that the worst days for their nation were over. It would have been easy for them to lapse into reassuring routine and think, "The LORD will do nothing, either good or bad" (Zephaniah 1:12). Perhaps these leaders thought this prophet who belonged to the royal line would give his high-society peers some welcome news of coming blessing, in spite of their continued refusal to obey the Lord. But they were in for a rude awakening!

2. Further details about Zephaniah are sparse and/or speculative.

We know nothing about this hidden prophet except what he reveals about himself in this book—and that's not much. We are provided with the names of his father, grandfather, great-grandfather, and great-great-grandfather. We are also told that he ministered during the reign of Josiah, who instituted a national religious reform whose chief features included a covenant renewal ceremony, a renovation of the temple, removal of idolatrous priests and worship, and a celebration of the Passover unequaled in previous history. Zephaniah's prophecy seems to indicate a time during Josiah's reign when such religious revival did not characterize the nation. Perhaps this implies a time before Josiah's reforms. Or perhaps it simply reveals that Josiah's reforms were nothing more than a veneer over a deep-rooted national apostasy that only a dramatic purging could cleanse.

We are provided no visual clues regarding the appearance of Zephaniah beyond the general description in *Ulpius the Roman*, which unhelpfully informs us that Zephaniah looked "like John the Theologian."[3]

Zephaniah's name means "the LORD hides" or "the LORD preserves," and may refer to the fact that the Lord protects those who humbly trust him. In Zephaniah 2:3 a synonymous verb (*s-t-r*) is used to express this idea of hiding or sheltering:

> Seek the LORD, all you humble of the land,
>> you who do what he commands.
> Seek righteousness, seek humility;
>> perhaps you will be sheltered [*s-t-r*]
>> on the day of the LORD's anger.

The idea of hiding or preserving may also refer to the situation surrounding Zephaniah's birth, during the years of evil King Manasseh. Faithful parents would surely pray during those days that the Lord would hide their children from the king, who had already shed so much innocent blood.[4] Whatever the referent, the fact that Zephaniah's name contains the idea of hiddenness is highly appropriate for this prophet who remains hidden away in the last few books of the Old Testament.

One other possibility concerning Zephaniah warrants discussion here. In the four-person genealogy provided by Zephaniah in the first verse of his prophecy is the intriguing name of his father—"Cushi." In Hebrew, "Cush" usually refers to "the lands of the Nile in southern Egypt, meaning Nubia and northern Sudan,"[5] and "Cushi" usually means "Cushite," or a person from those lands in northern Africa. The phrase "son of Cushi" in Zephaniah's genealogy, therefore, could possibly refer not to a person, but to an ethnic origin. This has led some scholars to argue that:

Zephaniah was of African descent and should be counted among other biblical characters from Africa—such as Simon of Cyrene (Matt. 27:32; Mark 15:21; Luke 23:26), the Ethiopian eunuch (Acts 8:27–39), the unnamed evangelists from Cyrene who proclaimed Christ in Antioch (11:20), and Simeon called Niger and Lucius of Cyrene in Antioch. (13:1)[6]

Also, the fact that Zephaniah mentions Cush two other times (Zephaniah 2:12; 3:10) may suggest that he perhaps had a personal interest in this area or people group. Arguing against this, however, is the fact that in the first of these other references (2:12) the Lord announces through his prophet that the Cushites "will be slain by my sword." It is difficult to understand why Zephaniah would go out of his way to associate himself with such a doomed group. Additionally, it would be extremely rare for the phrase "son of x" in a genealogy to refer to an ethnic group instead of a specific individual; and the other names in the genealogy are common Jewish names. Nevertheless, the debate over Zephaniah's racial background continues in scholarly circles.

3. Zephaniah was a contemporary of Jeremiah, Habakkuk, and perhaps Nahum.

Dates for Zephaniah's ministry are given in the vicinity of 627 BC. This would place him in or near the period of the ministry of Jeremiah (c. 627–580 BC), Habakkuk (c. 630 BC), and Nahum (c. 650 BC).[7] Each of these prophets was called by God to speak about a different facet of God's actions for and toward his people. Nahum saw the judgment to come upon Assyria, and Habakkuk struggled with God's future use of the Babylonians to judge his people. But Jeremiah and Zephaniah exposed the sin of God's people that merited the coming judgment.

Jewish tradition goes beyond an acknowledgment that Zephaniah and Jeremiah were contemporaries and suggests that Zephaniah was actually Jeremiah's teacher! The tradition suggests the relative importance of these two prophets by asserting that, when Jeremiah began to prophesy, "he limited his activity to speaking in the streets, whereas Zephaniah preached in the synagogue."[8] It is clear from the biblical text itself, however, that Jeremiah certainly was also active within the temple precincts (Jeremiah 7:2; 19:14; 26:2, 7, 9; 28:1, 5; 35:2, 4; 38:14).

4. The book of Zephaniah is never directly quoted in the New Testament.

Never being directly quoted in the New Testament is a dubious distinction Zephaniah shares with only Obadiah and Nahum. We can understand the absence of quotations from Obadiah because of its brevity (twenty-one verses). And the difficult content of Nahum perhaps contributes to its unquotability. But that there is no quotation from the three chapters of Zephaniah's prophecy is a little more difficult to comprehend.

However, although there are no direct quotations, there may, in fact, be allusions to Zephaniah in the New Testament. For example, Romans 14:11 and Philippians 2:10 refer to every knee bowing before the Lord. These passages may be referring to Zephaniah 2:11, which similarly talks about distant nations bowing down to the Lord.

Another such example may be Zephaniah 3:12, which refers to the "meek and humble" remnant who trust in the Lord. This possibly finds an echo in Jesus's call to the weary and burdened to find rest in him because he is "gentle and humble in heart" (Matthew 11:28–29). The words Jesus uses to describe himself are exactly the same words used in the Greek translation of Zephaniah 3:12, which suggests that Jesus is alluding to this verse to describe himself as the true remnant whose redemptive work brings about the rest he promises to those who trust in him.

A final example may be found in Peter's description of Jesus as the only true Israelite about whom one could say "no deceit was found in his mouth" (1 Peter 2:22). Perhaps when Peter said these words he had in mind the words of Zephaniah 3:13, which address a future day when Israel "will tell no lies" and "a deceitful tongue will not be found in their mouths."

These possible parallels, as well as the New Testament use of major themes found in Zephaniah (for example, the day of the Lord, living securely before judgment comes, corrupt leaders, etc.), force one to conclude that although Zephaniah is not specifically named in the New Testament, his ideas, and perhaps even some of his words, are.

5. Zephaniah begins his prophecy with a bang!

At the very beginning of his prophecy, Zephaniah records the Lord's declaration that he would, effectively, undo his work of creation! In 1:2–3, he says,

> "I will sweep away everything
>> from the face of the earth," declares the LORD.
>
> "I will sweep away both man and beast;
>> I will sweep away the birds in the sky
>> and the fish in the sea—
>> and the idols that cause the wicked to
>> stumble."
>
> "When I destroy all mankind
>> on the face of the earth," declares the LORD.

Notice the repeated sections at the beginning and the end:

- "'the face of the earth,' declares the LORD"
- man (Hebrew *'ādām*) / mankind (Hebrew *'ādām*)

The proposed destruction would rival that of the flood and uses the same terminology (Genesis 6:7). While "everything" will be swept away in God's judgment, only one created being is repeated—mankind. The divine purge is comprehensive in scope and ultimate in degree. And it is focused on human beings, those of high and low station, Israelites and non-Israelites. We must wait until the end of the last chapter for any glimmer of hope in the dark night of God's wrath and anger.

6. There is an extrabiblical book about Zephaniah.

There is a pseudepigraphical work entitled the *Apocalypse of Zephaniah*, dated between the first century BC and the second century AD, that "has been partially preserved in two separate manuscripts [Sahidic and Akhmimic] that come from the White Monastery of Shenuda near Sohag."[9] Clement of Alexandria also quotes this composition.

These surviving texts include brief descriptions of various visions experienced and recounted by Zephaniah. These include:

- "the fifth heaven," where crowned and enthroned angels sing hymns to God (Clement, *Stromata*, 5.11.77);
- a lawless soul punished and guarded by five thousand angels (Sahidic manuscript B, 1–7);
- a "great and broad place," surrounded by "thousands of thousands" (Sahidic manuscript B, 8–9);
- a burial scene (Akhmimic manuscript, 1:1–2);
- the seer's city from a lofty vantage point (Akhmimic manuscript, 2:1–9);
- angels who record all the good and evil deeds of human beings, which they will present at the gate of heaven (Akhmimic manuscript, 3:1–9);
- hideous angels who bring the souls of ungodly human beings to the place of their eternal punishment (Akhmimic manuscript, 4:1–10);
- the bronze gates of the heavenly city and glimpses of what lies beyond (Akhmimic manuscript, 5:1–6);
- the great angel, Eremiel, and the accuser in Hades (Akhmimic manuscript, 6:1–17);

- two manuscripts containing a record of the good and bad deeds Zephaniah had done throughout his entire life (Akhmimic manuscript, 7:1–11);
- scenes from a boat involving angels praising and praying with Zephaniah (Akhmimic manuscript, 8:1–5); and
- a great angel with a golden trumpet that he blew several times—three times to announce Zephaniah's triumph over the accuser and escape from Hades (Akhmimic manuscript, 9:1–5), once to open heaven to reveal the souls in torment (Akhmimic manuscript, 10:1–14), once toward heaven and once toward earth to call the righteous to prayer for those in torment (Akhmimic manuscript 11:1–6), and again toward heaven and toward earth as prelude to a description of the Lord's coming "to destroy the earth and the heavens" (Akhmimic manuscript, 12:1–8).

This composition no doubt owes its origin, as do most pseudepigraphical works, to the motivation to satisfy curiosities about so many biblical details that are left unanswered. These include details about eternal reward and eternal punishment, angels, the architecture and administration of heaven, etc. Unfortunately, these expansions remain largely unsubstantiated by biblical texts and remain just as hidden as details about our prophet.

7. In Jewish tradition, Zephaniah is associated with the Messiah's work of salvation.

There is a Jewish tradition that offers a perspective contrary to the biblical text, which presents Zephaniah as a prophet of the coming day of God's wrath. This Jewish tradition includes Zephaniah among a very select group of individuals involved with the coming day of God's salvation! The old rabbinic literature states that when the Messiah is about to begin his work of salvation, he will have a "council of fourteen" to assist him. This council will be comprised of seven "shepherds" and seven "princes." The princes are "the Messiah as the head, and Samuel, Saul, Jesse, Elijah, Amos, Zephaniah, and Hezekiah."[10]

While an interesting tradition, it remains unclear why it was thought the Messiah would need a council of any number to assist him, much less a council of fourteen. Nevertheless, this Jewish tradition reflects the high regard in which Zephaniah must have been held, and further stimulates our efforts to acquaint ourselves with this hidden prophet.

8. Zephaniah has his own holiday too!

On the calendar of feasts and fasts for the Greek Orthodox Church, Zephaniah's feast day is December 3 (on the Julian calendar, corresponding to December 16 on the modern Gregorian calendar).[11] In the book of the anniversaries of the martyrs and other saints commemorated by the Roman Catholic Church, the prophet Zephaniah is remembered on December 3 "in Judea."[12]

THE GOSPEL ACCORDING TO ZEPHANIAH

God had shown his people his love and care for them throughout their history. He had given them laws and guidelines to follow that would yield for them the fullest life possible. He had even gone so far as to provide a way for them to enjoy his presence among them, first by means of the tabernacle, then by means of the temple. But his people had essentially turned their backs on God. Other things had lured them away, and they no longer trusted in the Lord (Zephaniah 3:2). God had graciously sent them prophets to encourage them to return to the path of life, but God's people had accepted no correction and felt no shame for doing so (3:2, 5). Even their religious leaders—those who should have been working the hardest toward turning the people back to God—had themselves turned away from God (3:4). He had shown them that turning away from God and the path of life was tantamount to turning away from life itself. If they insisted on doing this, they would be renouncing their distinctiveness and choosing to be treated the same as the rest of the nations. Zephaniah brought them the news that if this was what they wanted, this was indeed what they would get. They would be judged by God along with everyone else. There was only one place where "shelter" could be found on the day of God's judgment, a day described as a time of wrath, distress, anguish, trouble, ruin, darkness, gloom, clouds, and blackness (1:15). That God should provide such a refuge at all reveals an extraordinary and incomprehensible mercy. But the good news is that he indeed holds out such a refuge—and that refuge is realized by means of humble trust in him (2:3).

The devastating judgment that would certainly come against God's people in 586 BC pointed toward a final divine judgment that is just as certainly coming. The apostle Paul tells us that God "has set a day when he will judge the world with justice by the man he has appointed" (Acts 17:31). That man, Jesus, is the only One who does not himself deserve judgment, and when he became flesh, his message echoed Zephaniah's.

Zephaniah foretold a coming divine judgment against sin. Only those who "seek the LORD" with humility and "do what he commands" will find shelter when that judgment comes. Of course, none of us consistently seek the Lord or do what he commands! There is only one human being who ever did. Jesus makes it clear that he is the only One who is truly "gentle and humble in heart" (Matthew 11:29), whose food it is to do the Father's will (John 4:34). The Father graciously counts Jesus's humble obedience as that of any of us who trust in him. Jesus is the shelter "on the day of the LORD's anger" that was prophesied by Zephaniah (2:3). In Jesus's own words: "Whoever hears my word and believes him who sent me has eternal life and will not be judged but has crossed over from death to life" (John 5:24).

Jesus, the only human being who didn't deserve divine judgment, has paid the price on the cross for all the rest of us who do. Anyone who refuses this payment for their sin is refusing the only escape from divine wrath on the coming day of judgment and is instead insisting on paying for their sin themselves. The good news is that God loves us so much that he became one of us in order to save us from the consequences of our sin. Zephaniah prophesied about a day when God's people would be glad and rejoice because the Lord would have taken away their punishment (Zephaniah 3:15). It would happen because of God's presence with them (3:15, 17). These prophecies are fulfilled by Jesus, who is "God with us" (Matthew 1:23). Jesus is "the Mighty Warrior who saves" (Zephaniah 3:17). He invites us to come to him humbly and trust him to rescue us.

WHY ZEPHANIAH SHOULD MATTER TO YOU

Zephaniah reminds God's people of the dangers that exist outside of the protective environs of fellowship with God. Apart from protection of "the Mighty Warrior who saves" lie the chaos that results from greed (Zephaniah 1:8), violence and deceit (1:9), oppression (3:1), injustice (3:3), and corruption (3:7). Contrary to these, God offers gracious abundance, love and truth, divine care, justice, and equity. These are available to all who enter into a relationship with God through faith in Jesus Christ. This ancient truth should matter to us because our lives both now and in the future hang on how we respond to it.

Outside this safety of God's protection against the consequences of sin are all of its corrosive and life-depleting effects. God has already provided the means for our deliverance from sin's penalty and power by means of Jesus's obedience and sacrifice. He is coming again to remove even the presence of sin. God will ultimately purge sin and its destructive effects from his creation once and for all. Those who are clinging to sin will be purged along with it. Those who have finally released their grip on it and have grabbed instead onto the divine hand of salvation extended to them will escape. Zephaniah's appeal still has traction today: escape while you can!

Those of us who have found refuge in God and have experienced the goodness of life in fellowship with him are nevertheless sometimes tempted by our associations and circumstances to wander off the path of life, if only for occasional day trips. We may think that by doing so we are giving ourselves a break from our otherwise bland lives. But this thinking is wrong on two levels. First, if we think life with God is bland, then we're not living it as he intends! I doubt the apostles Peter and Paul would describe their lives as bland! Bucking the values of the world and living counterculturally as a believer are about as far from accepted norms as one can get. Opening oneself up to cultural ostracism or ridicule is hardly going with the flow. And the true peace, security, contentment, meaning, purpose, and direction provided by the creator of life itself has no rival in the world of godless humanity.

Additionally, while we may believe true life exists beyond the bounds of divine guidelines, this is actually a lie foisted on believers by the father of lies. It is exactly the opposite of the truth. Life is not found outside of divine instruction; death is! When we wander outside the safety of the fortress of "the Mighty Warrior who saves" (Zephaniah 3:17), we expose ourselves to all the cancerous effects of sin that are inimical to life. The longer we expose ourselves to those effects, the more difficult it is for us to crawl back to the only place of safety. We need to help one another nurture the life God has for us in Christ so that our full appreciation of it is not inhibited by unsuspected scammers. The author of the book of Hebrews wrote to similarly encourage believers who had found refuge in Christ not to be lured away from the truth:

Let us hold unswervingly to the hope we profess, for he who promised is faithful. And let us consider how we may spur one another on toward love and good deeds, not giving up meeting together, as some are in the habit of doing, but encouraging one another—and all the more as you see the Day approaching. (Hebrews 10:23–25)

The "Day" that is approaching is none other than the day Zephaniah prophesied! There is no doubt that some who heard Zephaniah's prophecy of divine wrath thought it had nothing to do with them. They had everything going for them—ancestry, religious or political position, titles, wealth. Surely these objects of human desire would protect them from God's judgment. But those things would not protect them, and they will not protect us. There is only one thing that can—a relationship with God himself through faith in Jesus Christ. Jesus not only accomplished for us our deliverance *from* divine judgment; he also accomplishes for us our deliverance *into* true life in all of its richness—human life as the One who created it intended it to be. It is impossible to imagine anything that could matter more!

DISCUSSION QUESTIONS

1. The leaders in Zephaniah's day had gradually adopted the practices of the people groups around them until they had become indistinguishable from them. Why do you think the leaders were unaware this was happening? What could they have done to prevent it? What can you do to prevent it?

2. Zephaniah describes the human reaction to God's deliverance as singing, shouting, being glad, and rejoicing with all one's heart (3:14). Does that describe your own salvation experience? If not, what do you think might be keeping that from being true for you?

3. Do you look forward to the Lord's return, or do you fear it? Are you confident in your deliverance through faith in Jesus Christ, or do you have your doubts?

4. Do you want God to remove sin from the world, or would you like to play with your sin a little longer? What makes sinful behavior attractive to you? What do you think it offers to you that the life God wants for you does not?

5. In what do you place your confidence? Are you relying on some of the same things that the leaders of Zephaniah's day did? What is the status of your relationship with Christ? Is it growing deeper, or are you growing apart? What might be causing this?

6. How could your faith community "spur one another on toward love and good deeds ... and all the more as you see the Day approaching"? How can you rely on one another to avoid the obvious and not-so-obvious challenges to your life with Christ?

HAGGAI

AGEO PROPHETA

We leave Zephaniah, mulling over in our minds his message of refuge from divine judgment, and we pensively press ahead on our road trip through the hidden prophets. But we notice that the roadway has become uneven and broken, and it is not long until we find ourselves motoring along uncertainly on loose gravel. The buildings along the route are in a state of destruction and deterioration. There is evidence of loss and ruin all around us. We suddenly realize that we are moving through the aftermath of a war zone. The travel guides for this place describe a palace and temple; well-designed and maintained urban centers; and fertile, productive farmland. But that's not what we see here at all! Buildings have been reduced to rubble, debris is everywhere, with only sporadic and haphazard attempts at rebuilding. The look of resignation on the faces of the inhabitants suggests their unhappy acceptance of this new situation. Melancholy and anxiety hang almost visibly in the air.

Yet something seems to be going on up ahead. People are gathering around a lone figure who is speaking to them from atop the wreckage of a ruined structure. The man's name, we're told, is Haggai, and he is telling the crowd that things don't have to be like this, that, in fact, they *shouldn't* be like this. Haggai is telling them that the first thing necessary for their prospects to turn around is a refocusing of their priorities. They are, after all, the people of God. It is time for them to show their commitment to their relationship with that God by rebuilding his temple. We seem to have arrived on the scene at a pivotal point in this community's existence. We'll stay for a while and see what develops.

LITTLE-KNOWN FACTS ABOUT HAGGAI

1. Haggai is the first prophet to minister to God's people after their exile.

The very first words of Haggai's book fix the date of his prophecy "in the second year of King Darius." These seven words enable us to understand the context in which Haggai both lived and ministered. King Darius I (also called Darius Hystaspes) was the third king of the Persian empire,[1] and he came to power in 522 BC. The second year of his reign would therefore be 520 BC. God had been doing exciting things leading up to this year.

We learn from the books of 2 Chronicles (36:22–23) and Ezra (1:1–4) that already in 539 BC God had moved the heart of the first king of the Persian empire, Cyrus the Great, to make a proclamation throughout his realm that any Jews who wished to do so could return to Jerusalem from their exile in Babylon. The first group of exiles who took him up on his offer numbered 42,360 (Ezra 2:64).

However, the sweetness of their homecoming was significantly tempered by the bitterness of the realities confronting them. Adding to the daunting enormity of the required reconstruction was the opposition of the neighboring peoples. These groups initiated psychological warfare against the returned exiles in conjunction with a concerted letter-writing campaign to the Persian king in their attempts to delay or stall the efforts of the newly arrived Jews.[2] Testifying to the resolve of this determined group is the fact that in two short years after their return (Ezra 3:8–13, 536 BC), in spite of the many obstacles in their way, they had successfully prepared the site and completed the foundation for a new temple of God. But their resolve had limitations. They had their own needs to attend to. A societal infrastructure needed to be rebuilt as well. They needed to provide for themselves places to live, schools, shops, and cleared fields for planting. There was so much to do! And the neighbors' opposition to these other projects was nothing like their opposition to building the temple.

Consequently, the enthusiasm for the work on the temple waned and finally dissipated completely. For sixteen years, the foundation of the temple lay disregarded. Every day, people would walk past it and stifle the pricks of conscience that its neglect would produce. And every day, it became easier and easier to ignore.

Into this context, God called the prophet Haggai to prophesy. Haggai showed the returned exiles how the priority they were placing on rebuilding the temple reflected the priority they were placing on their relationship with God. The temple was the divinely designated place where God chose to dwell with his people. If this divine presence with them was of any importance to them at all, then they would have to realign their priorities and get to work rebuilding the temple.

2. All of Haggai's prophecies can be precisely dated to a four-month period.

Haggai's prophecies can be dated to a four-month period (sixteen weeks) in the second year of the reign of Darius I, the king of Persia (520 BC).

The first prophecy of Haggai is dated to "the second year of King Darius, on the first day of the sixth month" (1:1). This date corresponds to August 29, 520 BC.

The second prophecy of Haggai is dated to "the second year of King Darius, on the twenty-first day of the seventh month" (1:15–2:1). This date corresponds to October 17, 520 BC.

The third prophecy of Haggai is dated to "the twenty-fourth day of the ninth month, in the second year of Darius" (2:10). This date corresponds to December 18, 520 BC.

The final prophecy of Haggai is dated to "a second time on the twenty-fourth day of the month" (2:20). This date also corresponds to December 18, 520 BC.

These dates reveal that Haggai's prophetic ministry overlapped with that of Zechariah, who also began his ministry in "the second year of Darius" (1:1). However, Zechariah's ministry extended far beyond Haggai's. The final prophecies of Zechariah (chapters 9–14) are usually dated to at least 480 BC[3]—a full forty years after the last recorded words of Haggai.

3. Haggai may have been an old man at the time he prophesied.

Haggai asks the returned exiles, "Who of you is left who saw this house in its former glory? How does it look to you now? Does it not seem to you like nothing?" (Haggai 2:3). This question seems to at least hint that Haggai might be placing himself among those who saw the previous temple, for how else would he know how it seemed to them?[4] Admittedly, this is thin evidence, but if true, it would mean that Haggai was an old man at the time of his prophecy. The temple was destroyed in 587 BC, and Haggai's prophecies are dated to 520 BC. Even if Haggai was very young at the time of the exile, he would have to be in his seventies when he prophesied. Weak corroboration for this theory is provided by the brief description of Haggai found in the work known as *Ulpius the Roman*, which describes Haggai as "aged, round-bearded, hairy."[5]

Nevertheless, we must acknowledge that there is "no indication in the book that Haggai had ever been to Babylon or known anything of the exile."[6] A mediating position between these two views seems to have been adopted in *Lives of the Prophets*, which claims that "Haggai … came from Babylon to Jerusalem, probably as a youth" (14:1). However, it would be hard to imagine how a young prophet could have earned the respect and hearing that Haggai did. He is one of the very few prophets in the Old Testament to whom the people listen and respond with obedience!

4. Haggai's prophecy has traditionally been held in low regard by both Jews and Christians.

It has been said that, in Judaism, "Haggai is among the least prominent of all the prophetic collections" and that, indeed, "the book of Haggai plays no part in the traditional Jewish liturgical structure."[7] Perhaps this is because Haggai prophesied at a time when it is believed that the Spirit of prophecy was waning. This view is evident in one Jewish tradition that maintains that, unlike such a commanding prophet as Jeremiah, Haggai, "who lived after his time, retained only a trace of the old prophetic power."[8]

The almost embarrassing inadequacy attributed to the book of Haggai in Jewish legend also appears in connection with Haggai's traditional association with Daniel, whom Jews do not regard as a prophet. In Daniel 10:7, we read that Daniel had a vision that those with him did not see. One of those with him, so the legend goes, was Haggai. So then Daniel, "though not a prophet ... was found worthy to behold the vision,"[9] and Haggai, though he was a prophet, was evidently not found worthy to do so!

Christians, too, have neglected this biblical book. The reason for this may simply be because of the fact that this second-shortest[10] book of the Old Testament lies hidden along a rarely traveled biblical byway, tucked between its longer but similarly ignored neighbors Zephaniah and Zechariah. One has to be fairly intent on locating the book of Haggai in order to benefit from it, and finding it is not easy.

But there may be other reasons for its disuse. If prophecy is understood to be primarily concerned with clear predictions about the future, then Haggai's prophecy seems hardly to qualify. Only the last few verses regarding Zerubbabel seem to be Messianic. Of course, this view of prophecy is overly narrow and misses the Messianic focus of all of Scripture.[11] Those who regard the primary task of prophets as calling for social justice are also disappointed with the book of Haggai, for there is little in it that they find useful. But giving priority to God, as Haggai urges, can result in nothing less than a justice that reflects his own. No human construct can compare to that!

5. Some suggest that Haggai was not even this prophet's name!

We must admit that the book opens with none of the usual information about the prophet's father, grandfather, etc. He is simply described as "the prophet Haggai" (1:1). Added to this is the interesting fact that there is no other person in the entire Old Testament with this name. This has led some to propose that "Haggai" is not a proper name at all but rather a kind of title.[12] If so, what does the word *Haggai* mean, and why would it be applied to this prophet?

The word *Haggai* means "festival," and there could be several reasons why the term could have been applied to this prophet. The term may suggest that he was born on one of Israel's religious holidays.[13] Another possibility is that the term may signal the fact that he began his ministry on a festival day. We're told that he began prophesying on "the first day of the sixth month" (Haggai 1:1). The first days of each month were times for sacrifices and celebrations (Numbers 28:11–15). A third possibility is that the festive activity to which this title alludes is that surrounding the rebuilding of the temple. All of these possibilities make the likelihood of "Haggai" being a title rather than a proper name seem all but certain.

Against this, however, is the fact that Haggai is mentioned alongside of Zechariah in Ezra 5:1 and 6:14, and Zechariah is a very common name in the Old Testament. So it seems highly unlikely that in these passages a proper name for one person would be used in conjunction with something that is not a proper name for the other person.[14] That would be like saying that the two men who prophesied to the postexilic community were Zechariah and the "Festival Guy." We must conclude, therefore, that "Haggai" (like "Zechariah") is a proper name. Perhaps the lack of identifying familial connections only implies that Haggai was already well-known among his hearers.

6. Haggai might have been a priest.

The theory that Haggai was a priest rests on only a few slim pieces of evidence. The first piece dates to the first century AD and is found within the pseudepigraphical work entitled *Lives of the Prophets*. In the brief section of this composition that deals with Haggai, we are told that "when he died he was buried near the tomb of the priests, in great honor as were they" (14:2).[15] Being laid to rest "near" and in similar fashion to priests suggests Haggai might have been one as well. It is certainly true that other prophets, such as Jeremiah, were also priests, so it would not be surprising if Haggai proved also to be both. Added to this suggestion is the fact that the main concern of

Haggai's prophecy was the rebuilding of the temple—something that would have been the chief concern of any priest, whose responsibilities surrounded it.

One further piece of evidence can be adduced, but its salience is questionable. Many of the psalms give evidence of their use in formal worship services involving a worship leader or priest.[16] In the context of discussion regarding the priesthood of Haggai, therefore, it is suggestive that in some versions of the Old Testament (the Septuagint, the Vulgate, and the Peshitta), he is attributed with the authorship of Psalms 138 and 145–48.[17]

In the final analysis, these bits of data are no more than suggestive. It may, in fact, be the case that Haggai was a priest as well as a prophet, but this does not seem to have any bearing on the content of the prophecy that has been delivered to us.

7. Haggai has his own holiday too!

On the calendar of feasts and fasts for the Greek Orthodox Church, the feast day for the prophet Haggai (Aggaeus) is December 16 (on the Julian calendar, corresponding to December 29 on the modern Gregorian calendar).[18] In the book of the anniversaries of the martyrs and other saints commemorated by the Roman Catholic Church, the prophet Haggai is remembered on July 4. But perhaps as further evidence of the generally low regard in which this prophet is held, he does not enjoy exclusive attention on this day; instead, he shares this feast day with the prophet Hosea.[19] So as we remember Hosea when we're grilling burgers, we can offer a toast to Haggai with a glass of lemonade as well!

THE GOSPEL ACCORDING
TO HAGGAI

Haggai was not some religious idealist who ignored the pressing realities of his people in his preoccupation with some unrealistic utopian vision. He lived among them. He saw the devastation they faced each day. He knew and experienced the difficulties with rebuilding a life not just from scratch, but from well short of scratch. Clearing away the debris was a painful reminder of the consequences of their past sins. It was far easier to ignore that reality than to face it by attempting to rebuild the once glorious but then nonexistent temple.

But Haggai knew that the life of his people was bound up with their relationship with God. And that relationship with God was manifested physically by the temple that he had designated as his dwelling place among them. But that physical structure was always intended to represent the deeper, more personal dwelling place God desired with his people—their hearts. The fact that the returned exiles had let the progress of building the temple languish for decades could only mean that they had also allowed their spiritual relationship with God to languish as well. Haggai urged God's people to restore their relationship with God to a place of priority in their lives and to manifest that reality by resuming work on his temple.

In his prophetic vision, Haggai was shown amazing things concerning the temple that would further motivate its building. These things involved Zerubbabel (Haggai 2:20–23), who was the administrative governor of Judah and, more importantly, a son of David and the ancestor of the Messiah (Matthew 1:12). God said he would make Zerubbabel like his "signet ring" (Haggai 2:23). A signet ring had a raised design on its outer surface that could make impressions in soft surfaces such as wax. That impression guaranteed the authority, power, and trustworthiness of its owner. Haggai relays God's message that Zerubbabel, this descendant of David, is a powerful guarantee of the promises God made with regard to this new temple. These promises would indeed be realized when a later offspring of David would himself enter the temple, bringing the Father's glory and peace (Luke 19:41–46).

In the course of time, God would fulfill this promise and send his own Son so that he could dwell among his people in an even more personal and relatable way. He would send Jesus, called "Immanuel," meaning "God with us," to initiate the construction of a new kind of temple. This new temple brings to reality what the physical temple could only point toward. The critical actor in this new construction project is the One who correctly orients the entire building process (Ephesians 2:19–22). Each believer, aligned with Christ, interconnects with every other believer to become the living temple of God. Consequently, the temple is no longer a place where we visit God; rather, it is his very dwelling that we form as his people (1 Corinthians 3:16). In fact, building God's house and establishing it as a place of peace and blessing is another way of describing Jesus's redemptive work. He is using everyone who believes in him as a "living stone" in the construction of his "spiritual house" (1 Peter 2:4–5). The good news is that this new temple will never be destroyed because God himself is building it. All we need is the same thing the people of Haggai's day did—faith to trust in God's promises.

WHY HAGGAI SHOULD MATTER TO YOU

Haggai's message should matter to us because we may find ourselves in a very similar situation to the people of his day. Like them, we may acknowledge that our once energizing and vibrant spiritual house is in a sad state of repair. And the reasons for that situation may be similar to theirs as well. We may find ourselves weary of maintaining a godly lifestyle at a time when our neighbors would be much happier with us if we didn't. We may have allowed our legitimate personal concerns to illegitimately consume our thoughts of God. Or we may have simply allowed the numbing routine of daily life to drug us into lethargic apathy toward spiritual things.

Like the returned exiles, we might be spending our lives on what is transitory and life draining instead of what is eternal and life giving. God reminds his people then and now through his prophet Haggai that our only meaning and significance in life is inextricably tied to doing the work of God. That work involves allowing ourselves to be used by him to build the place that communicates to the whole world that God's presence is in our midst. God wanted the nations surrounding Israel to see the presence of their God not just in a shiny new temple but also in the obedient, trusting lives of his people. Are we as concerned that unbelievers see the presence of our God in our lives, his new temple?

Haggai's message to his people and to us today is that we need to get busy building. The Lord's message to us both is, "Be strong, all you people of the land … and work. For I am with you" (Haggai

2:4). God provides us with the energy, the tools, and the blueprints. And there is a job for everyone! We have the resources of an almighty God given freely to us so that we can make our own lives and our lives together a beautiful place for God to dwell. He is the source of life; he created it, and he knows how we can experience it to the fullest. So when God dwells within us richly, we'll know life in all of its richness.

But for us, just as it was for the people of Haggai's day, it will be difficult to keep ourselves from adopting the same values as those who don't know the Lord. We are continually told that fulfillment in life is found in the things we own, in the amount of money we have, in the leisure activities we can dream up, or in our professional titles or positions. But we must acknowledge that our own creator knows better. He reminds his people through Haggai where our true meaning, purpose, and fulfillment in life are found. Perhaps surprisingly, we find our own fulfillment in life when we focus on him and not on ourselves. And when we have adjusted our priorities so that we find our joy and contentment in being used by God to build up his spiritual house instead of our own houses, then we, too, will hear him saying to us, "From this day on I will bless you" (Haggai 2:19).

DISCUSSION QUESTIONS

1. Do you think Haggai's message applies to you? Are you busy building the Lord's temple? How does it change your perspective on the church when you realize it is God's new temple in which he dwells by his Spirit?

2. Haggai forced the returned exiles to face the fact that they had let building the temple slip down on their priority list. They had been busy instead building their homes and tending to their own affairs. They were not seeking first "his kingdom and his righteousness" (Matthew 6:33). That sort of thing was more like third or fourth on their list of things to do. What are some things you might be giving greater priority to than building the Lord's house? Why might that be?

3. Do you really believe that you will experience more fulfillment in life by doing what God wants instead of what you want? We know what the correct answer for this question should be, but what is really the case? Why do you think other things might provide a richer human experience? What might you be thinking (perhaps without being aware of it) that those things can provide for you that God cannot?

4. Haggai wanted his people to be aware that building the temple had great significance. It revealed their inner disposition toward God, and it also was the visible representation of the presence of God with his people. Can other people see that God is present with you? What might they see in the course of your day that would lead them to that conclusion?

5. We are always engaged in some sort of building. We might be building our careers, our reputations, our retirement funds, or our influence. What are you trying to build with your life? What does building those things require from you? How permanent are

the things you're building? Are those the things what you want to spend your life on?

6. What changes could you make in your life so that you become more actively engaged in building the Lord's house? How will you hold yourself accountable to make them?

ZECHARIAH

As long as we're in the neighborhood of Haggai, we should also pay a visit to Zechariah, who resides just next door. It is a unique situation to have two prophets speaking to the same group of people at about the same time about the same issue. Clearly rebuilding the temple has some serious implications! However, although Haggai and Zechariah are colleagues in ministry, we learn from the residents that their styles could hardly be more different. Haggai delivers straightforward messages whose lack of creativity and imagination has subsequently resulted in somewhat dismal reviews by both Christians and Jews.[1] We hear about an entirely different situation when it comes to Zechariah's prophecies. Those who have heard him speak report experiencing a rhetorical extravaganza of bizarre imagery and almost opaque pronouncements. And as apparent evidence for the veracity of this report, when we arrive in town, we encounter groups of people scratching their heads and discussing the possible meaning of the unusual things they've heard him talking about—things that include, among other things, horns, measuring lines, a stone with seven eyes, a flying scroll, a basket with a woman inside, and bronze mountains. If Zechariah's ministerial credentials weren't impeccable, one fears he might be discounted as unstable! There is no doubt that the main thrust of Zechariah's prophetic efforts, like Haggai's, is meant to encourage the returned exiles to rebuild the temple. Evidently, however, this Zechariah character is approaching his task from an entirely different angle. We'll extend our stay so that we can find out more about this fascinating guy and what unique perspective he is bringing to this reconstruction project.

LITTLE-KNOWN FACTS ABOUT ZECHARIAH

1. All Zechariahs are not the same.

The difficulties with developing a coherent understanding of Zechariah begin with his name. Although the appeal may be lost on contemporary readers, "Zechariah" was evidently a very popular name in biblical times. More than twenty-five people in the Bible share it. The name consists of two parts in Hebrew: a verb ("remembered"), rendered as *Zechar* in English; and the subject of the verb ("Yah," short for Yahweh), rendered as *iah* in English. The name, therefore, means "Yahweh remembered," and it is apparently a testimony to the answered prayers of the parents for a son. Clearly, the wide use of the name indicates the Lord was granting many requests for male offspring. But the name's popularity results in the occasional confusion of individuals who share it. Consequently, we cannot always be certain that the Zechariah mentioned in various biblical texts is the prophet Zechariah whose name attaches to this book.

This name problem surfaces already in connection with the information provided in the first verse. There we are informed that Zechariah is the son of Berekiah and the grandson of Iddo. One notices immediately the similarity between "Zechariah son of Berekiah" and the "Zechariah son of Jeberekiah" whom the prophet Isaiah called as a "reliable witness" (Isaiah 8:2). But this cannot be the same person. Isaiah prophesied at least forty years before the nation of Judah fell to the Babylonians in 586 BC, and our Zechariah prophesied to the returned exiles from 520–480 BC—at least one hundred years later!

Perhaps a similar problem is introduced by the gospel of Matthew. In Matthew's record of Jesus's denunciation of the teachers of the law and Pharisees, we find this intriguing historical allusion: "And so upon you will come all the righteous blood that has been shed on earth, from the blood of righteous Abel to the blood of Zechariah son of Berekiah" (Matthew 23:35). This statement summarizes the deaths of all the innocent victims in the Bible by referencing the first (Abel in Genesis) and the last (Zechariah in 2 Chronicles; 2 Chronicles being the last book of the Bible in the Jewish canon). However, in 2 Chronicles 24:20–22, the Zechariah who is mentioned is "Zechariah son of Jehoiada the priest." There are at least three options to consider with regard to this Zechariah. First, Jehoiada may have been a descendant of Berekiah, so "son/descendant of Jehoiada" and "son/descendant of Berekiah" may be different ways to refer to the same individual. Second, Jesus is referring to a disastrous end for our prophet that is not recorded elsewhere in the Bible.[2] A third possibility is that the Zechariah son of Berekiah to whom Jesus refers is a different Zechariah than the one for whom our prophetic book is named. That our Zechariah did not meet such an end is also suggested by the extrabiblical composition *Lives of the Prophets*, which states that "he died when he had attained a great age, and when he expired he was buried near Haggai" (15:6).

We are perhaps on firmer ground with respect to the reference to Zechariah son of Iddo in Ezra 5:1 and 6:14. The Hebrew word translated as "son" can also mean "descendant." This fact, in addition to the correct time frame and association with Haggai, makes it likely that these verses refer to our prophet. Moving slightly downward on the probability scale, though still in the very possible range, is the reference in Nehemiah 12:16 to a Zechariah in the priestly line of Iddo who returned from exile with Zerubbabel. Both Jewish and Christian traditions support this identification,[3] as does Zechariah's preoccupation with the temple.[4] Nevertheless, the identification remains uncertain.

2. We don't even know whether Zechariah was young or old when he prophesied.

We have already seen that *Lives of the Prophets* says that Zechariah "died when he had attained a great age" (15:6). Of course, this does not mean that he was already at a great age when he prophesied. But earlier in the same chapter we read, "Zechariah came from Chaldea when he was already well advanced in years" (15:1).

There are two pieces of evidence, however, that point in the opposite direction. The first is the description of Zechariah found in a text written by a monk named John in AD 993 and referred to as *Ulpius the Roman*. Here we find this terse verbal sketch of Zechariah: "youthful, clipped hair, good-looking, with a smiling and bright-eyed face, little short of looking like a boy."[5] This implies either that Zechariah was remarkably young looking for a man "well advanced in years" or that he was not so old after all. This latter option seems to be confirmed by a passing reference in the prophet's book itself. In Zechariah 2:3–4, we are told that when an angel who had been speaking with Zechariah was leaving, a second angel came to meet the earlier one and said, "Run, tell that young man, 'Jerusalem will be a city without walls because of the great number of people and animals in it.'" The content of this message is certainly what one would call "prophetic." The "young man," then, to whom the first angel is directed to run and deliver this message would appear to be the prophet Zechariah. While this identification would seem to settle the issue of Zechariah's age, it is not completely clear that the young man and Zechariah are indeed the same person. There is at least some possibility, for example, that the young man referred to is the "man with a measuring line in his hand" mentioned in 2:1.[6]

3. Zechariah hardly qualifies as a Minor Prophet!

The Minor Prophets bear that designation not because of any lesser significance of their messages but because of their length. It is surprising, therefore, that a book with fourteen chapters should be counted among their number. After all, the book of Daniel has only twelve chapters! This last datum, however, is only a consideration for Christians, who include Daniel among the prophets. In the Jewish canon, the book of Daniel is not listed among the prophets. It is found instead among the collection of biblical books called the Writings.

While the book of Zechariah holds the prize as the longest of the Minor Prophets, it just barely edges out the book of Hosea for that title, coming in at just thirteen verses longer. For all its length, however, Zechariah is among the least regarded of the Minor Prophets. Perhaps this low estimation is because of Zechariah's association with Haggai, whom we have already seen "is among the least prominent of all the prophetic collections."[7] Additionally, Zechariah (along with Haggai and Malachi) was considered by Jewish tradition to evidence "only a trace of the old prophetic power" manifested by the earlier prophets, such as Jeremiah.[8]

Because of its greater length and perceived limited prophetic power, therefore, the book of Zechariah sits as uncomfortably among his eleven brothers in this section of Scripture as a basketball player at a weightlifters' convention. He has a hard time blending in.

4. Many scholars agree that the prophecy of Zechariah may be two or even three books instead of one.

Critical scholarship is almost unanimous in declaring that the first eight chapters of Zechariah are from a different author and time period than the last six chapters.[9] It is only the first eight chapters, so these scholars assert, that are rightly to be credited to the sixth-century prophet Zechariah.[10] Some scholars believe there is even evidence to further subdivide chapters 9–14 and to attribute different authorship to chapters 9–11 and 12–14.[11] While division of Zechariah into three units has found comparatively less acceptance among modern scholars, the division of chapters 1–8 from 9–14 "is now very widely accepted, even by those who are generally regarded as being conservative in their views."[12]

It's fair to say that the evidence amassed for this conclusion seems at first glance to be overwhelming. It is noted, for example, that the two parts focus on different time periods. Chapters 1–8 deal with issues of immediate concern to the postexilic community, while chapters 9–14 deal more with events in the future. Additionally, the two parts show observable changes in writing style and vocabulary. For example, in chapters 1–8, historical persons and dates are significant; in chapters 9–14, however, no personal names or dates are found.[13] Often it is suggested that the author of the second part of Zechariah is none other than Jeremiah. This is based on Matthew 27:9–10:

> Then what was spoken by Jeremiah the prophet was fulfilled: "They took the thirty pieces of silver, the price set on him by the people of Israel, and they used them to buy the potter's field, as the Lord commanded me."

This quotation cannot be located in our canonical book of Jeremiah but seems rather to be a loose paraphrase of Zechariah 11:13:

And the LORD said to me, "Throw it to the potter"—the handsome price at which they valued me!
So I took the thirty pieces of silver and threw them
to the potter at the house of the LORD.

Though the combined weight of these details seems almost to
attain the status of proof, when they are considered individually, they
shed that weight quickly and dramatically. For example, that the two
parts of Zechariah seem to focus on different time periods is not
proof of anything. If Zechariah did minister over a long period (traditionally from 520–480 BC), then he would have spoken at widely
different time periods. And one could hardly consider it surprising
that prophecies uttered or written up to forty years apart would evidence differences of style and vocabulary. In addition, that chapters
1–8 and 9–14 focus on different things may simply be evidence of an
orderly mind grouping similar materials together. As Longman and
Dillard succinctly state:

If an ancient author separates material by literary
form (vision, oracle), subject (immediate issues vs.
distant), or other criteria (e.g., dated vs. undated),
this would seem from our Western vantage the
actions of a rational, orderly person. These items
scarcely in themselves provide an argument for
multiple authorship unless one implicitly adheres
to a rather foolish notion that any one author will
write only one kind of literature.[14]

Matthew's attribution to Jeremiah of a quotation seemingly from Zechariah may have a similarly straightforward explanation. Matthew may be combining Jeremiah's references to the potter (Jeremiah 18:1–10; 19:1–13) with Zechariah's (Zechariah 11:12–13), and simply referring to the better-known prophet. Or Matthew may be referring to a statement of Jeremiah not found among the canonical book of his prophecy.

Consequently, each detail of the argument against the unity of Zechariah's prophecy, when considered individually, is unpersuasive. The proposal for multiple authorship raises interesting questions, but "the attention it has received seems to outweigh its importance."[15] Every piece of evidence adduced to support it can be as easily used to argue for reading the book as a unity.[16]

5. Zechariah's prophecy is difficult to understand.

Though the subject matter and focus of chapters 1–8 are different from chapters 9–14, both sections contain major interpretive difficulties. The major part of the first section consists of eight visions. Because Zechariah had all of these visions during a single night, they are usually referred to as his "night visions"—and they are bizarre! They include

> 1. a man mounted on a red horse among myrtle trees in a ravine (1:8–17);
> 2. four horns and four craftsmen (1:18–21);
> 3. a man with a measuring line in his hand (2:1–13);

4. Joshua the high priest standing before the angel of the Lord, with Satan standing at his right side to accuse him (3:1–10);

5. a solid gold lampstand with a bowl at the top and seven lamps on it; and two olive trees (4:1–14);

6. a flying scroll (5:1–4);

7. a basket with a lead cover and a woman inside (5:5–11); and

8. four chariots coming out from between two bronze mountains (6:1–8).

The second section (chapters 9–14) hardly brings any relief to the beleaguered reader. One is confronted with pronouncements of future judgments (9:1–8; 12:1–9) and blessings (10:1–12) involving the coming of the Lord as Israel's righteous and victorious king (9:9–17; 14:1–21). These future judgments and blessings are conceptually combined in images of two shepherds (11:4–17) weeping for "the one they have pierced" (12:10–14; 13:7–9) and a sin-cleansing fountain (13:1–6).

This barrage of theologically loaded imagery has led ancient as well as modern exegetes to express frustration in their attempts to understand it. Jerome, the early church scholar and exegete (347–420), apparently finding the prophecy of Zechariah to be virtually impenetrable by his interpretive devices, declared it to be *liber obscurissimus* (the most obscure book).[17] Later, the highly esteemed eleventh-century Jewish commentator Rabbi Shlomo Yitzchaki (known by the acronym Rashi) declared, "We shall never be able to discover the true interpretation until the teacher of righteousness arrives."[18] When that teacher of righteousness finally did arrive, the hidden meaning of these once impenetrable and obscure prophecies finally began to come into focus.

6. The book of Zechariah is quoted or alluded to in the New Testament more often than any other Minor Prophet.

Not only is Zechariah the most quoted by the New Testament of all the Minor Prophets,[19] but the passion narratives of the Gospels quote from chapters 9–14 of Zechariah more than any other portion of the Old Testament.[20] Just a few of these familiar references include:

- Matthew 21:5 and John 12:15 (from Zechariah 9:9)
Say to Daughter Zion,
    "See, your king comes to you,
gentle and riding on a donkey,
    and on a colt, the foal of a donkey."

- Matthew 26:31 and Mark 14:27 (from Zechariah 13:7)
I will strike the shepherd,
    and the sheep of the flock will be scattered.

- Matthew 27:9–10 (from Zechariah 11:12–13)
They took the thirty pieces of silver, the price set on him by the people of Israel, and they used them to buy the potter's field, as the Lord commanded me.

- John 19:37 (from Zechariah 12:10)
They will look on the one they have pierced.

Why the book of Zechariah has the distinction of being the most quoted Minor Prophet in the New Testament remains unclear. Perhaps it is because of Zechariah's focus on the larger spiritual realities pictured by the temple, spiritual realities that would ultimately be realized by the One who refers to himself as "this temple" (John 2:19). Perhaps it is because Zechariah's message of hope ultimately points toward the coming of the One in whom "the nations will put their hope" (Matthew 12:21). Whatever the reason, the New Testament writers found in Zechariah's prophecy abundant foreshadowing of the coming of the Messiah just two biblical books later!

7. Zechariah uses shocking imagery to point toward the coming Messiah.

With imagery that would alarm and upset his hearers, Zechariah points unmistakably to a future Messiah who would fulfill everything the Old Testament institutions and offices foreshadowed. Perhaps the most powerful example of this is found in only a few verses in chapter 6. In 6:9–11, Zechariah is instructed to do something *unthinkable*: set a silver and gold crown on the head of the high priest, Joshua.

Clearly, this is confusing two distinct offices. High priests don't wear crowns; kings do! When an attempt to confuse these two offices occurred during an earlier time, there were serious and disastrous consequences. At that time, King Uzziah had attempted to perform a priestly function by entering the temple to burn incense on the altar. Immediately, the Lord struck him with leprosy—a condition with which he was afflicted until the day he died (2 Chronicles 26:16–21). So to similarly confuse the two offices of priest and king once again (this time in the opposite direction), by having a priest wear a king's crown, would surely have created unease at the very least. This explains Zechariah's need to reiterate the reality of this new, unusual situation, investing it with even more features: "He will be clothed with majesty and will sit and rule on his throne. And he will be a priest on his throne. And there will be harmony between the two" (Zechariah 6:13). The *high priest*, Zechariah reveals, will wear a crown, be clothed in majesty, and sit and rule on a throne. There will be harmony between the offices of priest and king.

This would not be a royal privilege that Joshua the high priest would enjoy among the returned exiles. It rather symbolically pointed forward to One coming in the future who would combine the two offices of priest and king in himself. This explains the New Testament's quotation of Zechariah more than any other Minor Prophet! The gospel writers recognized Jesus as "the man whose name is the Branch" who would "build the temple of the LORD" (Zechariah 6:12–13).

The temple he would build is not the temple of Zechariah's day. That building only symbolized the temple this coming One would be constructing. This symbolism-fulfilling temple would be nothing less than the kingdom of God, ruled by "a high priest, who sat down at the right hand of the throne of the Majesty in heaven, and who serves in the sanctuary, the true tabernacle set up by the Lord, not by a mere human being" (Hebrews 8:1–2).

8. Zechariah has his own holiday too!

On the calendar of feasts and fasts for the Greek Orthodox Church, the feast day of Zechariah (Zacharias) is February 8 (on the Julian calendar, corresponding to February 21 on the modern Gregorian calendar).[21] In the book of the anniversaries of the martyrs and other saints commemorated by the Roman Catholic Church, the prophet Zechariah is remembered on September 6.[22] This same source reports that Zechariah "returned in his old age from Chaldea to his own country, and lies buried near the prophet Aggeus [Haggai]."

THE GOSPEL ACCORDING TO ZECHARIAH

While Haggai focused on the inner spiritual reality that the temple rebuilding signified, Zechariah focused on the outer spiritual reality it signified. Zechariah insisted that this rebuilding project was not some pointless and pedestrian effort by a ragtag group of nostalgic survivors who hoped that this would somehow reconnect them to the glory days of the past. Rather, he asserted, this rebuilding had profound, worldwide significance because it communicated, just as symbolically as Zechariah's prophecy, redemptive realities that God would accomplish by means of the coming Messiah.

Everything about the temple prophetically signified the salvation God would bring about by means of Jesus Christ. Its sacrificial rituals symbolically foreshadowed the removal of sin ultimately achieved by Christ (Zechariah 5:5–9; 13:1–6). Its liturgies reflected the relationship between "the king over the whole earth" and those from "many nations" who "will be joined with the LORD" (2:11; 8:20–23; 14:9, 16).

The high priest at the center of the temple sacraments, who offered the sacrifices that cleanse God's people and sustain their relationship with him, points ineluctably toward the coming high priest beyond compare who would offer himself to secure an eternal, unbreakable relationship between God and all those who by faith avail themselves of his perfect sacrifice (3:8–9; 6:9–13). Of course, such a self-sacrifice could achieve this outcome only if the high priest had no sin of his own to atone for. So, in an amazing demonstration of grace-filled condescension, the coming high priest would be the holy God himself who would become flesh and make his dwelling among us (John 1:14). This coming high priest would therefore combine in himself the offices of high priest and king.

The purifying power of this coming high priest–king will be so comprehensive that it will eventually extend over the whole earth (Zechariah 9:10; 14:9). All sin and its effects will be removed from the entire earth so that even household cooking pots will be holy (14:20–21). In that coming day, the whole earth will be God's temple, for "his rule will extend from sea to sea and from the River to the ends of the earth" (9:10).

The temple the returned exiles were rebuilding pointed toward all of these things, though that remained largely hidden to them. The significance of these prophecies began to unfold at the birth of the prophesied Branch, who would bring about this worldwide temple building (Zechariah 6:12). Jesus referred to himself as a temple (John 2:19); that is, he became in his person the fulfillment of everything the temple foreshadowed. He is the dwelling of God in our midst.

Through him, we have access to God. It is his sacrifice "once for all" that obtains for us an "eternal redemption" (Hebrews 9:12). Jesus is therefore the ultimate temple. All those who unite with him by faith are "living stones" in this temple (1 Peter 2:5; Ephesians 2:20–22). The good news is that it is not too late for additions! The temple is still being built. And it includes living stones from every nation, tribe, people, and language. It could include you too.

WHY ZECHARIAH SHOULD MATTER TO YOU

The prophecy of Zechariah should matter to us for the same reason it mattered to the returned exiles. In both cases, God is communicating something enormously profound by means of these construction projects. And in both cases, remembering the deeper implications of the task we're engaged in will keep us from flagging in our efforts as we face the challenging work ahead of us.

Zechariah reminded the postexilic community of God's people that God's temple was a means of communicating divine truth to the world. In the New Testament, the apostles remind the redeemed community of God's people that they, too, are engaged in a temple-building project that is intended to communicate divine truth to the world. The apostle Peter, for example, tells us that we are "being built into a spiritual house" (1 Peter 2:5). This spiritual house, or temple, has always been the place where God caused his presence to dwell among his people.

The apostle Paul scolded a faith community that had apparently forgotten this essential truth by asking them with some exasperation,

"Don't you know that you yourselves are God's temple and that God's Spirit dwells in your midst?" (1 Corinthians 3:16). Because the believers in Corinth had forgotten the deeper reality that should have defined and directed their quotidian activities, they had dropped the ball, or hammer, with regard to their temple-building responsibilities.

Our union with Jesus Christ by faith makes us living pictures to the world of the God who dwells in our midst. What does the temple we are building say to unbelievers about the God we say that we serve? Do they see a loving, just, holy, and gracious God—in short, do they see Jesus? Or do they see a temple like the one in Zechariah's day, one that has hardly anything yet erected on its foundation?

Zechariah's admonishment to "let your hands be strong so that the temple may be built" (8:9) finds traction in believers' lives as we participate in God's grand temple-building enterprise. We do this by consciously seeking to expand the church by the power of the Holy Spirit. As we utilize the construction tools God has placed in our hands (that is, our spiritual gifts, talents, resources, and opportunities) to communicate the good news of Jesus Christ with our words, actions, and emotions, we are effectively joining in the divine construction work of building God's temple. And as God brings each new believer into his kingdom, the temple rises on its foundation one living stone at a time (1 Peter 2:5).

Only when your eyes are opened to the larger spiritual realities that too often flicker indistinctly on the edge of our consciousness will the significance of Zechariah's words dawn on you. In those moments of clarity, this biblical book will matter to you, and your enthusiasm for the world-encompassing construction work of divine redemption will be reenergized!

DISCUSSION QUESTIONS

1. Zechariah showed that the offices and functions of the high priest, Joshua, and the civil leader, Zerubbabel, would be combined in a coming priest-king. How does understanding Jesus as both high priest and king help you better understand his redemptive work?

2. The returned exiles were encouraged in their work by being reminded that what they were doing had a significance that transcended their own place and time. How do your efforts in the church transcend your own place and time? What eternal realities do you demonstrate by means of your participation in God's work in the world?

3. Have you ever thought of your service to God in terms of spiritual temple building? If you have, what do you perceive as your role in this task? Are you an architect or a carpenter, a foreman or a laborer?

4. The temple was physically constructed in a way that visibly communicated truths about God. God uses his church today for the same purposes. How can God's temple today visibly communicate truths about him? How does your faith community communicate those truths? How could an unbeliever see them (as well as hear about them)?

5. Building the temple required resources. It required people, time, skill, commitment, materials, and money. What kinds of resources does the church need to build God's new temple? What resources has God already provided? How do we access those resources?

MALACHI

We leave Haggai and Zechariah to their shared and fruitful ministry of encouragement as we return to our road trip through the hidden prophets of the Bible. We have to travel a significant distance down the timeline—about two or three generations—before we reach our next, and final, stop on the tour. When we finally arrive in the region of Malachi, we can't help but see that circumstances in Jerusalem are greatly improved over those at our last stop. Tremendous progress has been made! The walls of the city have been rebuilt, and as we pass through the perimeter, we immediately notice that the temple is now completed on its site. We observe the divisions of priests and Levites busy about their tasks. The smoke of the regular, daily animal sacrifices hangs heavy in the air, scented by the accompanying incense offerings. By all external appearances, everything looks as it should.

But striking up a conversation with a local merchant at the bazaar, we soon learn that in the minds of many, things are not at all as they should be. We're informed that God's people are getting more than a little impatient for him to do something. God had made all sorts of promises regarding this postexilic community and this new temple. Those promises seemed to imply a world-shaking manifestation of God's power and glory that would include the long-awaited exaltation of his people and the judgment of their enemies. And God's people had believed those promises! But now years and years had gone by and nothing seemed to be happening. They were not exalted among the nations. In fact, they were hardly noticed by the dominant world powers on whose good graces, it seemed, they owed their continued existence! Did God still love them? Had God given up on them? Maybe, some were thinking, God really did no longer love them. Maybe he had given up on them. And if God apparently felt that way about *them*, did it make any sense for them to continue to honor *him*?

This lack of confidence in God's care for his people was manifesting itself in two major ways. First, their worship of God had become stale and insincere. Their worship was sputtering along now as a result of a sort of spiritual inertia rather than heartfelt devotion. People were even attempting to spice up their unfulfilling worship by introducing new ideas and practices that were foreign to the Scriptures. But even this wasn't working. A second way their lack of confidence in God's care was becoming evident was by an observable reciprocal lack of care for one another. They were becoming like how they pictured God to be: unloving and callous to the needs and desires of others.

In the midst of this sullen, dispirited group, we hear the voice of Malachi rising above the grumbling. He is speaking with energy, candor, and passion. He is pointing out the errors in his countrymen's thoughts and actions. He seems to us to be making a strong case, but it is unclear from the faces of those gathered around whether his words are penetrating their collective funk. Our realization of the parallels to our own contemporary religious situation and our curiosity about the outcome for this community impel us to hang around to hear the rest of the story.

LITTLE-KNOWN FACTS ABOUT MALACHI

1. Malachi may be a description and not a personal name at all!

The word "Malachi" is a combination of the Hebrew word מַלְאָךְ (mal'āk), meaning "messenger," and the pronoun suffix יִ (î), meaning "my." "Malachi," therefore, means "my messenger." This raises the question of whether Malachi is a proper name at all. It may simply be a general designation for an otherwise unnamed person whom God used to deliver his message during a time when "only a trace of the old prophetic power" remained.[1]

Evidence supporting this view includes the fact that nowhere in the book is Malachi referred to as a prophet! However, the word "messenger" *is* found in a couple of places: once in 2:7 in the description of a priest as a "messenger of the LORD Almighty," and once in 3:1 where the Lord announces, "I will send my messenger [מַלְאָכִי malā'kî], who will prepare the way before me." Is this book, then, which comes immediately before the coming of Jesus in the Gospels, a fulfillment of this promise to send "my messenger"?

Further support for the interpretation "my messenger" instead of "Malachi" may come from the Septuagint, the ancient Greek translation of the Old Testament. The Greek word for "messenger" is ἄγγελος (*angelos*). The Septuagint translates the Hebrew word מַלְאָכִי in Malachi 1:1 as ἀγγέλου αὐτοῦ, "his messenger." So, the Septuagint regarded "Malachi" in this verse not as a proper name, but as a general designation. Also, if Malachi were indeed a proper name, it seems odd that it would not be found anywhere else in the entire Bible. Therefore, some conclude, "it would seem most probable that the writer is unknown, an editor of the Book of the Twelve having bestowed the name Malachi upon the author of this anonymous collection of prophecies on the basis of the phrase in 3:1. For convenience, however, he is generally referred to as Malachi."[2]

This evidence may seem persuasive, but there are strong counterarguments. For example, the significance of the fact that Malachi is nowhere called a prophet in this book pales dramatically when one realizes that among the other Minor Prophets, Hosea, Joel, Amos, Obadiah, Jonah, Micah, Nahum, and Zephaniah are not called prophets anywhere in their books either! Yet Joel is called a prophet by the apostle Peter (Acts 2:16), and Jonah is called a prophet by Jesus (Matthew 12:39). That Malachi is not called a prophet in his book is hardly an argument against his being one. Also, that Malachi is not mentioned anywhere else in the Bible signifies nothing when one considers that the same is true for Amos, Obadiah, Nahum, and Zephaniah.

The word "Malachi" is situated at the beginning of the book in precisely the place one would expect to find it if it were, in fact, a proper noun. Most scholars, therefore, conclude that Malachi is indeed a proper name for a man about whom Scripture has nothing else to say beyond what we find in this book that bears his name.[3]

2. Some traditions suggest that Malachi is another name for Ezra, or even Mordecai!

The problems with identifying Malachi resurface in connection with certain traditions that equate him with Ezra. The English translation of Malachi 1:1 in Targum Jonathan (dated c. 50 BC) is "A prophecy. The word of the LORD to Israel through Malachi, whose name is Ezra the scribe."[4] This identification of Malachi with Ezra also appears in a Jewish tradition that asserts, "The complete resettlement of Palestine took place under the direction of Ezra, or, as the Scriptures sometimes call him, Malachi."[5]

It is true that the identification of Malachi as Ezra is at least chronologically feasible. The prophecy of Malachi is usually dated to the same time or slightly before Ezra's return to Jerusalem,[6] which is usually dated to around 458 BC.[7] But to conclude from this synchronicity that these two individuals were actually the same person is far more than such meager evidence warrants.

The conclusion that Malachi is actually Mordecai is based on even slimmer evidence. It seems to rest entirely on the similarity of the meaning of the Hebrew text at the end of the book of Esther and an alternative understanding of the meaning of the name Malachi.[8] In Esther 10:3, Mordecai is described as "second in rank to King Xerxes." If the name Malachi is incorrectly regarded as deriving from the Hebrew word "king" (מלך) instead of "messenger" (מלאך), then Malachi could be construed as meaning "the kingly one" and, therefore, another designation for Mordecai. We can safely place this suggestion in the "fascinating but utterly impossible" file.

3. Some scholars suggest that Malachi should not even be a separate prophetic book.

The attack on Malachi's independent existence continues with a more serious charge. Some scholars assert that rather than being a separate prophetic book, Malachi should be considered as simply a continuation of the prophecy of Zechariah! The strongest evidence for this assertion centers on the phrase "An oracle. The word of the LORD" (מַשָּׂא דְבַר־יְהוָ ,ה). These three Hebrew words are found together in this order at the beginning of Zechariah 9:1, Zechariah 12:1, and Malachi 1:1—and nowhere else in the entire Bible! This seems to support the conclusion, made by some, that the entire book of Malachi "would appear to be the third section of a collection of prophecies (Zech. 9:1–Mal. 4:6) which at some point have been added to the work of the sixth-century prophet Zechariah, and the third section having been given a separate identity under the name of Malachi."[9]

One might well ask what would motivate someone in the first place to separate Malachi from the rest of Zechariah if it really were originally a continuation of it. The answer usually offered to this possible objection is that whoever finally edited the canonical collection of the Minor Prophets would have wanted to end up with "the sacred number of twelve prophets."[10]

The logic of this assertion is just a bit faulty, however. To say that the use of the same words necessarily implies the same person spoke them is about as sensible as saying that because Alexander Graham Bell and Elisha Gray both registered patents for the telephone in 1876 within one hour of each other, they must be the same person. Add to this the observation that the theological content and historical background of the book of Malachi "are entirely different" from those of Zechariah,[11] and the argument against the independence of Malachi melts away as fast as manna in the sunshine (Exodus 16:21).

4. Traditional materials suggest that Malachi was a young man.

The biblical materials give us nothing to go by in this regard. As is usually the case in these situations, traditions develop to fill in the gaps.

The pseudepigraphical composition *Lives of the Prophets* records a tradition that Malachi died while still a young man: "And while he was still a young man he was added to his fathers in his own field" (16:4).

A much later source, though perhaps dependent on *Lives of the Prophets*, is the tenth-century text usually referred to as *Ulpius the Roman*. In this work, a tradition is recorded that describes Malachi as "youthful" and "good-looking."[12]

5. One of Malachi's prophecies will be fulfilled by Elijah!

Malachi prophesied that God will "send the prophet Elijah to you before that great and dreadful day of the LORD comes. He will turn the hearts of the parents to their children, and the hearts of the children to their parents; or else I will come and strike the land with total destruction" (Malachi 4:5–6). This Elijah to come is identified as the "messenger" referred to earlier in Malachi 3:1: "I will send my messenger, who will prepare the way before me. Then suddenly the Lord you are seeking will come to his temple; the messenger of the covenant, whom you desire, will come."

The New Testament clearly finds the fulfillment of both of these verses in Malachi in John the Baptist. Mark 1:2 quotes Malachi 3:1 to introduce the activity of John the Baptist. Similarly, in Matthew 11:7–14, Jesus brings together both Malachi 3:1 and 4:5–6 in his description of John the Baptist. So there is no question that John fulfilled Malachi's prophecy; the question, rather, is *how* John fulfilled it, particularly with regard to Malachi 4:5–6—especially in light of the fact that John the Baptist denied being Elijah in John 1:21!

Malachi 3:1 identifies one messenger as preceding a second messenger, who is described as the Lord, the messenger of the covenant. This nicely describes John the Baptist, whose message preceded that of the Lord himself, who effectuated the new covenant. The more difficult passage to contend with is Malachi 4:5–6. It raises a few questions, such as, what does Elijah have to do with this? How is this prophecy fulfilled? And, what does this have to do with John the Baptist?

It seems that Malachi's Elijah and John the Baptist share a number of features that lead one to conclude that Malachi's prophecy is indeed fulfilled by John the Baptist.[13] John the Baptist spent much time in the wilderness (Mark 1:4), as did Elijah (1 Kings 17:2–6; 19:3–9). John the Baptist was a lone voice (Mark 1:3), as was Elijah (1 Kings 19:3–9). Most importantly, Elijah preached repentance (1 Kings 18:37), which was precisely what John the Baptist did (Mark 1:4).

Understanding the "turning the hearts of the parents to their children" and vice versa requires the knowledge of a common literary device called a merism. A merism involves citing two ends of a spectrum to include everything in between. An example from contemporary English is to search "high and low"—meaning, of course, to search those two places and everywhere in between as well. So when Malachi says that the coming Elijah will turn the hearts of parents to their children and children to their parents, he is using a merism to communicate a "unified obedience to the faith on the part of everyone."[14] This is exactly what the angel of the Lord told Zechariah that his son, John the Baptist, would do (Luke 1:16–17). So, though John the Baptist denied being the literal Elijah (who did not die and for whom Jewish legend had a further role), John nevertheless fulfilled Malachi's prophecy about the coming Elijah by carrying out functions similar to those that characterized the historical Elijah.

What were these Jewish beliefs about the further role the Elijah of the past had yet to play before judgment day—a role that involved turning the hearts of the parents back to their children? Rabbi Louis Ginzberg explains:

> On that day the children of the wicked who had to die in infancy on account of the sins of their fathers will be found among the just, while their fathers will be ranged on the other side. The babes will implore their fathers to come to them, but God will not permit it. Then Elijah will go to the little ones and teach them how to plead on behalf of their

fathers. They will stand before God and say: "Is not the measure of good, the mercy of God, larger than the measure of chastisements? If, then, we died for the sins of our fathers, should they not now for our sakes be granted the good, and be permitted to join us in Paradise?" God will give assent to their pleadings, and Elijah will have fulfilled the word of the prophet Malachi; he will have brought back the fathers to the children.[15]

Such elaborate and creative exegetical contortions are easily obviated, however, by recognizing the fulfillment of Malachi's prophecy in John the Baptist, as Jesus plainly states (Matthew 11:7–14).

6. Some scholars and traditions regard Malachi's prophetic power as inadequate.

We have already seen that Jewish tradition holds that Haggai, Zechariah, and Malachi "retained only a trace of the old prophetic power."[16] The fact that Malachi sits at the end of this waning power curve only makes his situation that much worse. This may explain why *Lives of the Prophets* felt the need to have Malachi's prophecies buttressed by an angelic echo: "Moreover, whatever he himself said in prophecy, on the same day an angel of God appeared and repeated it" (16:3).

This view of Malachi's relative powerlessness lives on among some contemporary scholars. Consider, for example, the remarks of W. Neil:

Malachi cannot be reckoned among the great prophets. He does not share the profound and original insights into the nature and purpose of God which were given to men like Amos, Jeremiah, and Second Isaiah. He lived at a time when prophetic utterances were no longer accepted without question as direct communications from Yahweh.... He had to argue his case in a way that his predecessors in the heyday of classical prophecy had never been obliged to do.[17]

In Malachi's defense, one can hardly fault the prophet for how his message is received. By that standard, one would be forced to judge Jesus himself as a failure! As for Malachi lacking "profound and original insights," his insight into the fact that the behavior of the people of God should reflect attributes of God himself seems fairly profound and insightful. Perhaps what one considers profound and insightful has more to do with the hearer than the speaker.

7. Malachi has his own holiday too!

On the calendar of feasts and fasts for the Greek Orthodox Church, Malachi's feast day is January 3 (on the Julian calendar, corresponding to January 16 on the modern Gregorian calendar).[18] In the book of the anniversaries of the martyrs and other saints commemorated by the Roman Catholic Church, the prophet Malachi is remembered on January 14 "in Judea."[19]

THE GOSPEL ACCORDING TO MALACHI

Malachi spoke to a spiritually dry and struggling people. Their single most important foundational principle for their identity and motivation in life was in serious doubt. Did God still love them? Malachi addresses this pivotal question already in verse 2 of his prophecy. He addresses it again at the end as well (4:5). Malachi communicates God's message that the "day of the LORD"—the day when the enemies of God and his people will be judged and when those who honor God will finally receive their promised reward—is indeed coming and that it will be heralded by the coming of Elijah. The ultimate demonstration of God's love and the beginning of the unfolding of the promised day of the Lord are realized in the coming of Jesus Christ.

It is hardly a coincidence that a book that raises the question of God's love for his people is immediately followed by the Gospels, which narrate God's physical demonstration of that love! The last of these Gospels says it plainly: "For God so loved the world that he gave his one and only Son, that whoever believes in him shall not perish but have eternal life" (John 3:16). This physical revelation of divine love comes to ultimate expression in Jesus's willingness to bear God's wrath against our sin. As the apostle Paul writes, "God demonstrates his own love for us in this: While we were still sinners, Christ died for us" (Romans 5:8). Jesus has therefore removed all possible doubt regarding God's love for us. But we can be excused if we wonder how this could be.

After all, another aspect of God's love, promised by Malachi, is that God's enemies and the enemies of his people will be judged and those who honor him will be blessed. Unfortunately, Malachi makes it abundantly clear that God's people were not honoring him. In fact, they were doing exactly the opposite! They were offering God their castoffs instead of their best (Malachi 1:6–14). Their religious leaders were leading people astray with teachings contrary to God's word (2:1–9). They were communicating exactly the wrong message about the God they said they followed by their unfaithfulness to each other (2:10–16), by depriving the vulnerable of justice (2:17–3:5), by withholding their tithes (3:6–12), and by saying it was futile to serve God (3:13–15). This all sounds uncomfortably familiar to our own situation! And all these behaviors and attitudes seem to place these people on the "enemies of God" side of the day of the Lord rather than on the "those who honor God" side. Consequently, it would seem that judgment is merited instead of blessing.

So where is there room for the gospel, or the good news? How can God promise blessing when all of us deserve judgment instead? The answer, again, is because of Jesus Christ. Jesus perfectly honored the Father. He gave his life in his Father's service (Philippians 2:8). He lived by the word of God (Matthew 4:4) so completely that he is even called "the Word" (John 1:1). "He was faithful to the one who appointed him" (Hebrews 3:2). He exercised justice and was the One the prophet foretold who would proclaim justice to the nations (Matthew 12:18). He gave himself as our sacrifice (Hebrews 9:26). He served God so completely that he could say his food was to do the will of him who sent him (John 4:34).

In short, Jesus is everything one must be to merit God's blessing on the day of the Lord. He is the One heralded by John the Baptist, whom Jesus identifies as the Elijah whose presence was a harbinger of that day (Matthew 11:14). The good news is that the perfectly obedient, God-honoring life of Jesus is credited to all who unite with him by faith! That's because the perfectly disobedient, God-dishonoring life of all the rest of us has been credited to Jesus on the cross. God's "day of the Lord" judgment has already been experienced by those who trust in Christ. All that remains is the blessing. This is truly an amazing love and good news for all who understand it and embrace it!

WHY MALACHI SHOULD MATTER TO YOU

Anyone who reads this hidden prophet will probably recognize a familiar spiritual struggle. God's people had grown impatient waiting for the fulfillment of his promises. The stories they heard from their grandparents about the amazing things God had done in the past seemed barely two unicorns shy of fairy tales. Did God still love them like that? Was he still interested in them at all? Had he forgotten about them? It had been a long time since they had even heard a prophetic voice, much less seen any unmistakable manifestation of divine power exercised on their behalf. Maybe it was foolish to continue to believe that God had a glorious future planned for them.

These questions and doubts may sound familiar because we have them too. God's people today have waited a long time for him to fulfill his promises of a glorious future. It's been two thousand years! The stories we read in the Bible seem fantastic, incredible, almost mythical. Yes, Jesus was an amazing demonstration of God's love. But does God still love us like that? Is he still interested in our pedestrian lives? Has he forgotten about us? Maybe the voices of the surrounding culture are right. Maybe it's foolish to keep looking to the heavens for the return of a Savior who will make all things new.

Malachi's message should matter to God's people today because he speaks to the doubts and uncertainties we know and struggle to keep at bay. It is so difficult to continue to honor God when doing so requires a long and continually assailed faith. That's why God does not call us to travel this road on our own. He has sent his Spirit to each believer to give us the strength to live in determined and resolute faith and obedience, even during the long dry spells when our circumstances may lead us to question God's continuing love for us.

The Spirit reminds us that our true security, direction, and fulfillment in life are not found, after all, in our circumstances. They are found instead in our relationship with God. Leaning into that relationship with God is how we honor him and appropriate the full life he desires for us. And God honors us in return by granting us undeserved salvation, vibrant life, and promises of even greater things in the future. In response to these divine favors, we delight in that undeserved salvation, experience that vibrant life as we align our efforts with God's purposes, and enjoy his current blessings in the sure knowledge that even more are coming. Malachi's message matters because it refocuses our attention on the only place where human experience can find its fullest possible contentment—in relationship with the God who always has and always will love us more than we could ever know.

DISCUSSION QUESTIONS

1. What doubts or fears about God do you wrestle with? Do you believe God loves you? Or do you think he has forgotten about you? How do these doubts or fears keep you from experiencing the full life God wants for you? What can you do to change that?

2. Is your faith more dependent on the circumstances around you or on your relationship with God? Which do you spend more of your time developing?

3. What does your life say to the people around you about what you think God is like? We are supposed to be conforming to the image of Jesus (Romans 8:29). How would people describe Jesus if they only had you to go by?

4. Would you say that your life brings honor to God? Or have the demands and busyness of your life pushed God out of the picture? What one thing could you do today to bring honor to God? Where can you find the strength to do it?

5. What would you say is the most worthwhile thing to spend your life on? Are you spending the precious years of your life on that? Do the things you have decided to spend time on bring you the contentment you hope for?

CONCLUSION

We've come to the end of our road trip through the hidden prophets. And as we see Malachi recede from sight in our rearview mirror, we have the opportunity to reflect on our experiences before we return to the more populated and frequently traveled regions of Scripture. Who knew that such fascinating characters existed just beyond the awareness of most biblical tourists? As is usually the case when we visit foreign lands, we soon become aware that the joys, concerns, hopes, and struggles of the people we meet are really not that much different from our own. We can always learn a lot about ourselves and our own situations by paying attention to them and their circumstances. And we realize that we have indeed learned a lot about ourselves and our own situations as a result of our time with the hidden prophets. We have been changed. We have grown as human beings and, more specifically, as Christian human beings.

Each prophet has given us at least one souvenir perspective to take with us. For some, that souvenir will be getting to know the prophet as an individual instead of just the title of a biblical book. For others, it will be the glimpse of the gospel in the prophet's words that finds its fulfillment in Jesus. Still others might find new insight into the implications of the prophet's message for their lives.

Specifying what souvenir any one of us should take away from each prophet would seem to be just as illegitimate as specifying for travelers what they should take away from any of the small towns they visit. For each traveler through these hidden prophets, the souvenir perspective will be just as individual and unique as they are. But one thing is true for all of us who have visited these neglected biblical boroughs. As we leave these back roads behind and merge back onto the interstate heading for the Gospels, we are all better equipped to intelligently and fruitfully navigate those narratives. Not only that, but our memory cards are filled with pictures of a part of the biblical world that people rarely see. As we share our many memories and experiences with family and friends, these hidden prophets may not remain hidden much longer. And that would be a very good thing indeed!

RESOURCE ABBREVIATIONS

BDB   Brown, Francis; S. R. Driver; and Charles A. Briggs. *The New Brown-Driver-Briggs-Gesenius Hebrew and English Lexicon.* Peabody, MA: Hendrickson, 1979.

CANE   *Civilizations of the Ancient Near East.* Edited by J. Sasson. 4 vols. Peabody, MA: Hendrickson, 1995.

COS 1   *Canonical Compositions from the Biblical World.* Vol. 1 of *The Context of Scripture.* Edited by William W. Hallo and K. Lawson Younger Jr. Leiden, Netherlands: E. J. Brill, 1997.

COS 2   *Monumental Inscriptions from the Biblical World.* Vol. 2 of *The Context of Scripture.* Edited by William W. Hallo and K. Lawson Younger Jr. Leiden, Netherlands: E. J. Brill, 2000.

EBC   *The Expositor's Bible Commentary.* Rev. ed. Edited by Tremper Longman III and David E. Garland. 13 vols. Grand Rapids, MI: Zondervan, 2006–2012.

HALOT   *The Hebrew and Aramaic Lexicon of the Old Testament.* Edited
           by L. Koehler, W. Baumgartner, and J. J. Stamm. Translated
           and edited under the supervision of M. E. J. Richardson. 4
           vols. Leiden, Netherlands: E. J. Brill, 1994–1999.

IDB   *The Interpreter's Dictionary of the Bible.* Edited by G. A.
           Buttrick. 4 vols. Nashville, TN: Abingdon, 1962.

JETS   *Journal of the Evangelical Theological Society.*

NIB   *The New Interpreter's Bible.* Edited by Leander Keck, et al.
           12 vols. Nashville, TN: Abingdon, 1994–2002.

NIDOTTE   *The New International Dictionary of Old Testament Theology
           and Exegesis.* Edited by Willem A. VanGemeren. 6 vols.
           Grand Rapids, MI: Zondervan, 1997.

NIVAC   The NIV Application Commentary.

ZECOT   *Zondervan Exegetical Commentary on the Old Testament: A
           Discourse Analysis of the Hebrew Bible.* Edited by Daniel I.
           Block. Grand Rapids, MI: Zondervan, 2013.

ZIBBC   *Zondervan Illustrated Bible Backgrounds Commentary.* Edited
           by John H. Walton. 5 vols. Grand Rapids, MI: Zondervan,
           2009.

NOTES

INTRODUCTION

1. Accessed off Arizona Highway 77.

2. Accessed off California Highway 180 or 198.

3. Accessed off Kansas Highway 9.

4. Accessed off California Highway 111.

HOSEA

1. This tradition is referenced in Louis Ginzberg, *The Legends of the Jews*, 7 vols., trans. Henrietta Szold (Philadelphia: Jewish Publication Society, 1909–38), 6:356, n. 22.

2. Ginzberg, *Legends*, 6:356, n. 21.

3. One tradition (Ginzberg, *Legends*, 6:355, n. 20) even maintains that Hosea prophesied for ninety of those years!

4. D. R. A. Hare, *The Old Testament Pseudepigrapha*, 2 vols., ed. James H. Charlesworth (Garden City, NY: Doubleday, 1985), 2:385.

5. Hare, *Pseudepigrapha*, 2:391.

6. Ginzberg, *Legends*, 4:261.

7. *HALOT*, 1:275.

8. M. Daniel Carroll R., "Hosea," *EBC*, 8:228.

9. For a fuller list of examples of Hosea's use of alliteration, assonance, word plays, and unique words, see A. A. MacIntosh, *Hosea, International Critical Commentary* 23A (Edinburgh: T&T Clark, 1997), lxiv, 586–93.

10. This delightful example is provided by Rick Steves, *Rick Steves' German Phrasebook and Dictionary* (Emeryville, CA: Avalon Travel, 2003), 269.

11. *BDB*, 170.

12. See *CANE*, 1:45–46. See also Raymond Westbrook, *Old Babylonian Marriage Law, AfO* 23 (Horn, Austria: Ferdinand Berger & Söhne, 1988), 48–49.

13. For a convenient listing of the feasts and fasts on the Orthodox calendar, see "Calendar of Saints, Feasts, and Readings in the Orthodox Church," Greek Orthodox Archdiocese of America, www.goarch.org/chapel/calendar/.

14. See the Roman Martyrology provided online by the *Boston Catholic Journal* at www.boston-catholic-journal.com/roman-martrylogy-in-english/roman-martyrology-july-in-english.htm#July_4th.

JOEL

1. *HALOT*, 3:985.

2. Louis Ginzberg, *The Legends of the Jews*, 7 vols., trans. Henrietta Szold (Philadelphia: Jewish Publication Society, 1909–38), 4:64–65.

3. Ginzberg, *Legends*, 6:229, n. 46.

4. For a helpful list of dates proposed by various scholars and the evidence that supports them, see Raymond B. Dillard and Tremper Longman III, *An Introduction to the Old Testament*, rev. ed. (Grand Rapids, MI: Zondervan, 2006), 414.

5. Robert C. Stallman, "אַרְבֶּה," in *NIDOTTE*, 1:492, states: "If these terms do not represent developmental stages, they may refer to different species, colors, regional names, or simply be synonyms used rhetorically."

6. Rachel Nuwer, "A Plague of Locusts Descends upon the Holy Land, Just in Time for Passover," Smithsonian.com, March 6, 2013, www.smithsonianmag.com/science-nature/a-plague-of-locusts-descends-upon-the-holy-land-just-in-time-for-passover-779476/?no-ist.

7. K. A. Kitchen, "The Battle of Qadesh—the Poem, or Literary Record (2.5A)," *COS* 2:34. For other examples of locusts used to describe armies, see Stallman, "אַרְבֶּה," *NIDOTTE*, 1:492.

8. This parallel is cited by Mark W. Chavalas, "Joel," pp. 43–53 in John H. Walton, *Zondervan Illustrated Bible Backgrounds Commentary* (Grand Rapids, MI: Zondervan, 2009), 45; and discussed more fully by Victor Avigdor Hurowitz, "Joel's Locust Plague in Light of Sargon II's Hymn to Nanaya," *Journal of Biblical Literature* 112 (1993): 597–603. See also Alasdair

Livingstone, "A Hymn to Nanaya with a Blessing for Sargon II (1.141)," *COS* 1:473.

9. Hurowitz, "Hymn to Nanaya," 599.

10. Hurowitz, "Hymn to Nanaya," 603.

11. "Calendar of Saints, Feasts, and Readings in the Orthodox Church," Greek Orthodox Archdiocese of America, www.goarch.org/chapel/calendar/.

12. See the Roman Martyrology provided online by the *Boston Catholic Journal* at www.boston-catholic-journal.com/roman-martyrology-in-english/roman-martyrology-july-in-english.htm#July_13th.

13. See p. 20.

14. See "Gush Halav" at https://info.goisrael.com/en/gush-halav-287461.

15. The Benedictine monks of St. Augustine's Abbey, *The Book of Saints: A Dictionary of Persons Canonized or Beatified by the Catholic Church*, 5th ed. (New York: Thomas Y. Crowell, 1966), 378.

16. D. R. A. Hare, *The Old Testament Pseudepigrapha*, 2 vols., ed. James H. Charlesworth (Garden City, NY: Doubleday, 1985), 2:392.

17. E. A. W. Budge, ed. and trans., *The Book of the Bee* (Oxford: Clarendon, 1886), available online at https://ldsfocuschrist2.files.wordpress.com/2012/03/syriac-book-of-the-bee-budge.pdf.

18. Note how Joel links the coming day of the Lord with the locust plague that foreshadows it by using almost identical language (2:10–11).

AMOS

1. R. F. Gribble, "Tekoa," in *The Zondervan Pictorial Encyclopedia of the Bible*, 5 vols., ed. Merrill C. Tenney (Grand Rapids, MI: Zondervan, 1976), 5:612.

2. Hans Walter Wolff, *Joel and Amos: A Commentary on the Books of the Prophets Joel and Amos*, trans. Waldemar Janzen, S. Dean McBride, Jr., and Charles A. Muenchow; ed. S. Dean McBride Jr. (Philadelphia: Fortress, 1977), 124; and Thomas E. McComiskey and Tremper Longman III, "Amos," *EBC*, 8:356.

3. Louis Ginzberg, *The Legends of the Jews*, 7 vols., trans. Henrietta Szold (Philadelphia: Jewish Publication Society, 1909–38), n. 20.

4. See, for example, Thomas E. McComiskey, "Amos" (1436–37) and "Micah" (1467); Leon Wood, "Hosea" (1407); and Geoffrey W. Grogan, "Isaiah" (1041–44); in *Zondervan NIV Bible Commentary, Volume 1: Old Testament*, eds. Kenneth L. Barker and John Kohlenberger III (Grand Rapids, MI: Zondervan, 1994).

5. Ginzberg, *Legends*, 4:261.

6. Ginzberg, *Legends*, 6:358, n. 32.

7. "Calendar of Saints, Feasts, and Readings in the Orthodox Church," Greek Orthodox Archdiocese of America, www.goarch.org/chapel/calendar/.

8. See the Roman Martyrology provided online by the *Boston Catholic Journal* at www.boston-catholic-journal.com/roman-martrylogy-in-english/roman-martyrology-march-in-english.htm#March_31st.

9. Ginzberg, *Legends*, 4:261–62. Indeed, the biblical account of Jeroboam's victory over the Arameans is attributed by Jewish tradition to his refusal to act against Amos: "Israel's victory over the Aramaeans, under king Joash [i.e., Jehoash, 2 Kings 13:25], was the reward of this king for his refusal to listen to the accusations brought against the prophet Amos by Amaziah" (Ginzberg, *Legends*, 6:348, n. 22).

10. Ginzberg, *Legends*, 4:261–62; *The Lives of the Prophets*, 7:1–3; E. A. W. Budge, ed. and trans., *The Book of the Bee* (Oxford: Clarendon, 1886), available online at https://ldsfocuschrist2.files.wordpress.com/2012/03/syriac-book-of-the-bee-budge.pdf, p. 44; and Roman Martyrology, *Boston Catholic Journal*, www.boston-catholic-journal.com/roman-martrylogy-in-english/roman-martyrology-march-in-english.htm#March_31st.

OBADIAH

1. D. R. A. Hare, *The Old Testament Pseudepigrapha*, 2 vols., ed. James H. Charlesworth (Garden City, NY: Doubleday, 1985), 2:392.

2. Louis Ginzberg, *The Legends of the Jews*, 7 vols., trans. Henrietta Szold (Philadelphia: Jewish Publication Society, 1909–38), 5:195, n. 72; and 6:375, n. 104.

3. See, for example, James D. Nogalski, *The Book of the Twelve: Hosea–Jonah* (Macon, GA: Smyth & Helwys, 2011), 367: "Attempts to identify a prophet with specific persons named Obadiah mentioned elsewhere in the Bible have not met with critical concurrence."

4. See, for example, Jeffrey J. Niehaus, "Obadiah," in *Obadiah, Jonah, Micah, Nahum, and Habakkuk*, vol. 2 of *The Minor Prophets: An Exegetical and Expository Commentary*, ed. Thomas E. McComiskey (Grand Rapids, MI: Baker Academic, 1993), 502: "It has been traditionally held … that the Obadiah who wrote this prophecy was the same Obadiah in Ahab's service who encountered Elijah (1 Kings 18:3–16). But modern commentators have been reluctant to identify the author as that Obadiah. The traditional view may be correct, however."

5. Ginzberg, *Legends*, 6:355–56, n. 20.

6. Ginzberg, *Legends*, 4.189.

7. Ginzberg, *Legends*, 4:241, quoting Proverbs 19:17.

8. Ginzberg, *Legends*, 6:345, n. 7.

9. Ginzberg, *Legends*, 6:343, n. 1.

10. Jeffrey H. Tigay and Alan R. Millard, "Seals and Seal Impressions," *COS* 2:200 (2.70Q).

11. Ginzberg, *Legends*, 4:240 and 6:344, n. 6. Consider, especially, the expansion of the biblical narrative regarding God's address to Eliphaz in Job 42:7–8 that is found in Ginzberg, *Legends*, 1:422: "God rebuked Eliphaz, and said: 'Thou didst speak harsh words unto My servant Job. Therefore shall Obadiah, one of thy descendants, utter a prophecy of denunciation against thy father's house, the Edomites.'"

12. Ginzberg, *Legends*, 6:344, n. 6.

13. Ginzberg, *Legends*, 6:344, n. 6.

14. Ginzberg, *Legends*, 5:361, n. 332.

15. Ginzberg, *Legends*, 1:20–21.

16. S. Cohen, "Edom, Edomites," *IDB*, 2:24.

17. S. Cohen, "Edom, Edomites," *IDB*, 2:24: "This territory ... received the name of Edom, 'the red region,' from the red rocks and soil that abound everywhere through it."

18. John R. Bartlett, *Edom and the Edomites* (JSOTSup 77; Sheffield: JSOT Press, 1989), 41.

19. Daniel I. Block, ed., *Obadiah*, in *Exegetical Commentary on the Old Testament: A Discourse Analysis of the Hebrew Bible*, vol. 27 (Grand Rapids, MI: Zondervan, 2013), 106.

20. Bartlett, *Edom and the Edomites*, 157–61.

21. For informed speculation about this little-known people group, see Bartlett, *Edom and the Edomites*, 172–74.

22. For references to Edom's reputed wisdom (beyond what is mentioned in Obadiah 8), see Nogalski, *Hosea–Jonah*, 386.

23. Bartlett, *Edom and the Edomites*, 40.

24. For an outline of the various conflicts, see S. Cohen, "Edom, Edomites," *IDB*, 2:24–26.

25. For an analysis of other possible, though less likely, dates and circumstances, see Block, *Obadiah*, 23–24.

26. Block, *Obadiah*, 106: "[Obadiah] links the demise of Edom with the 'day of YHWH' that is approaching for all nations, so that the Edomites function as a representative of all the nations arrayed against YHWH and his people."

27. "Calendar of Saints, Feasts, and Readings in the Orthodox Church," Greek Orthodox Archdiocese of America, www.goarch.org/chapel/calendar/.

28. Bartlett, *Edom and the Edomites*, 186: "The destruction of Edom was a parable of the destruction of the nations as a whole; indeed, the destruction of the peoples might be pictured as taking place in Edom itself. Edom could be named to symbolize a world empire, seen in opposition to God."

JONAH

1. G. W. Van Beek, "Gath Hepher," *IDB*, 2:356.

2. John H. Walton, "Jonah," *ZIBBC* 5:101: "A reference to Jonah the son of Amittai in 2 Kings 14:25 places the setting for the book of Jonah between 790 and 760 BC."

3. Louis Ginzberg, *The Legends of the Jews*, 7 vols., trans. Henrietta Szold (Philadelphia: Jewish Publication Society, 1909–38), 6:351, n. 38; 6:318, n. 9.

4. D. R. A. Hare, *The Old Testament Pseudepigrapha*, 2 vols., ed. James H. Charlesworth (Garden City, NY: Doubleday, 1985), 2:392.

5. Ginzberg, *Legends*, 4:246.

6. Ginzberg, *Legends*, 5:146, n. 42.

7. Ginzberg, *Legends*, 4:253.

8. John H. Walton, "Jonah," *EBC*, 8:455.

9. Kevin J. Youngblood, *Jonah*, *ZECOT*, 51:30.

10. Walton, "Jonah," *EBC*, 8:455.

11. Walton, "Jonah," *EBC*, 8:455, 478.

12. Youngblood, *Jonah*, 51:31.

13. Ginzberg, *Legends*, 4:246–47.

14. Ginzberg, *Legends*, 6:351–52, n. 38.

15. Ginzberg, *Legends*, 4:249.

16. Ginzberg, *Legends*, 4:249–50.

17. Ginzberg, *Legends*, 4:252.

18. Ginzberg, *Legends*, 4:253.

19. "Calendar of Saints, Feasts, and Readings in the Orthodox Church," Greek Orthodox Archdiocese of America, www.goarch.org/chapel/calendar/.

20. See the Roman Martyrology provided online by the *Boston Catholic Journal* at www.boston-catholic-journal.com/roman-martrylogy-in-english/roman-martyrology-september-in-english.htm#September_21st. Where exactly this "land of Saar" is located is difficult to determine. It is interesting to note, however, that *Lives of the Prophets* mentions two potential parallels. In 10:2, Jonah is said to have sojourned in Sour, "a territory (inhabited by) foreign nations." Then later, after Jonah had returned to the land of Judah, 10:9 informs us that he sojourned in "the land of Saraar." The obvious similarity between Saar and both Sour and Saraar suggests the same place, which nevertheless, remains unidentified.

MICAH

1. Bruce K. Waltke, *A Commentary on Micah* (Grand Rapids, MI: Eerdmans, 2007), 3.

2. Bruce K. Waltke, "Micah," in *Obadiah, Jonah, Micah, Nahum, and Habakkuk*, vol. 2 of *The Minor Prophets: An Exegetical and Expository Commentary*, ed. Thomas E. McComiskey (Grand Rapids, MI: Baker Academic, 1993), 594.

3. Tremper Longman III and Thomas E. McComiskey, "Micah," *EBC*, 8:496.

4. Louis Ginzberg, *The Legends of the Jews*, 7 vols., trans. Henrietta Szold (Philadelphia: Jewish Publication Society, 1909–38), 6:355, n. 20.

5. Ginzberg, *Legends*, 6:343, n. 1.

6. Ginzberg, *Legends*, 6:355, n. 20, cites a tradition that identifies "the prophet Micah with Micaiah the son of Imlah who prophesied during the time of Jehoshaphat (1 Kings 22:8)."

7. *COS* 2:285 (2.117A).

8. *COS* 2:288 (2.117C).

9. *COS* 1:467 (1:137).

10. *COS* 2:296 (2.118E).

11. Waltke, *Commentary on Micah*, 7.

12. *COS* 2:303 (2:119B).

13. Waltke, "Micah," 628.

14. Waltke, "Micah," 631.

15. "Calendar of Saints, Feasts, and Readings in the Orthodox Church," Greek Orthodox Archdiocese of America, www.goarch.org/chapel/calendar/.

16. See the Roman Martyrology provided online by the *Boston Catholic Journal* at www.boston-catholic-journal.com/roman-martrylogy-in-english/roman-martyrology-january-in-english.htm#January_15th.

NAHUM

1. The only legend recorded in Ginzberg's *Legends* (6:314, n. 56; 6:373, n. 100) is from Seder 'Olam 20, which asserts that Joel, Nahum, and Habakkuk were contemporaries of Manasseh.

2. Richard Coggins and Jin H. Han, *Six Minor Prophets through the Centuries* (Malden, MA: Wiley-Blackwell, 2011), 17.

3. See Tremper Longman III, "Nahum," in *Obadiah, Jonah, Micah, Nahum, and Habakkuk*, vol. 2 of *The Minor Prophets: An Exegetical and Expository Commentary*, ed. Thomas E. McComiskey (Grand Rapids, MI: Baker Academic, 1993), 765–66. *Lives of the Prophets* 11:1 seems to combine the second and fourth options: "Nahum was from Elkesi on the other side of Isbegabarin."

4. Cited by John Lowden, *Illuminated Prophet Books: A Study of Byzantine Manuscripts of the Major and Minor Prophets* (University Park, PA: Pennsylvania State University Press, 1988), 52.

5. For this and other disparaging comments regarding Nahum's prophecy, see, for example, Walter A. Maier, *The Book of Nahum: A Commentary* (Grand Rapids, MI: Baker, 1980), 70–84. Among the various charges against Nahum that Maier records are that he ignores Israel's sins, that he shows gloating hatred and malicious joy, that he is a prophet of incipient Judaism, that he is a false prophet, that he is opposed to other prophets, and that he reflects pan-Babylonian eschatology.

6. See "Prophet Nahum," Orthodox Church in America, http://oca.org/saints/lives/2007/12/01/103452-prophet-nahum; and "Saint Nahum, Prophet," Communio (Roman Catholic Church), http://communio.stblogs.org/index.php/2013/12/saint-nahum-prophet/.

7. These horrendous acts are spelled out in all their gruesomeness by Erika Belibtreu, "Grisly Assyrian Record of Torture and Death," *BAR* 17.1 (1991), 52–61, 75. This article is available online at http://faculty.uml.edu/ethan_Spanier/Teaching/documents/CP6.0AssyrianTorture.pdf. See further descriptions of Assyria's atrocities by James Bruckner, *Jonah, Nahum,*

Habakkuk, Zephaniah (NIVAC; Grand Rapids, MI: Zondervan, 2004), 28–29.

8. Bruckner, *Jonah, Nahum*, 183.

9. Bruckner, *Jonah, Nahum*, 137–38.

10. Diodorus Siculus, *The Library of History of Diodorus of Sicily*, trans. C. H. Oldfather, vol. 1 (London: William Heinemann, 1933), 441.

11. George P. Badger, *The Nestorians and Their Rituals* (London: Joseph Masters, 1852), 1:78, 79; cited my Maier, *Nahum*, 119.

12. Sir Henry Rawlinson, *The History of Herodotus* (London: John Murray, 1862), 448 n., cited by Maier, *Nahum*, 126.

13. See, for example, Maier, *Nahum*, 52–62.

14. Longman, "Nahum," 775.

15. *The Revised Common Lectionary: The Consultation on Common Texts* (Nashville, TN: Abingdon, 1992), 9.

16. "Calendar of Saints, Feasts, and Readings in the Orthodox Church," Greek Orthodox Archdiocese of America, www.goarch.org/chapel/calendar/; and the Roman Martyrology provided online by the *Boston Catholic Journal* at www.boston-catholic-journal.com/roman-martrylogy-in-english/roman-martyrology-december-in-english.htm#December_1st.

17. David Israel, "Kurdish Jews Scrambling to Save Prophet Nahum's Crumbling Tomb in ISIS Territory," Jewish Press, August 3, 2016, www.jewishpress.com/news/breaking-news/kurdish-jews-scrambling-to-save-prophet-nahums-crumbling-tomb-in-isis-territory/2016/08/03/.

HABAKKUK

1. Bethzouchar is identified as a town five to six miles southeast of Bethlehem. See D. R. A. Hare, "The Lives of the Prophets: A New Translation and Introduction," in *The Old Testament Pseudepigrapha*, ed. James H. Charlesworth (Garden City, NY: Doubleday, 1985), 393, n. 12a.

2. Louis Ginzberg, *The Legends of the Jews*, 7 vols., trans. Henrietta Szold (Philadelphia: Jewish Publication Society, 1909–38), 6:346, n. 10.

3. Marvin A. Sweeney, ed., *Micah, Nahum, Habakkuk, Zephaniah, Haggai, Zechariah, Malachi*, vol. 2 of *The Twelve Prophets* (Collegeville, MN: Liturgical, 2000), 454.

4. S. Szikszai, "Elisha," *IDB*, 2:91.

5. *HALOT*, 1:287.

6. For a description and picture of this rather uncomely sculpture, see Richard Coggins and Jin H. Han, *Six Minor Prophets through the Centuries* (Malden, MA: Wiley-Blackwell, 2011), 45.

7. Cited by John Lowden, *Illuminated Prophet Books: A Study of Byzantine Manuscripts of the Major and Minor Prophets* (University Park, PA: Pennsylvania State University Press, 1988), 52.

8. Ginzberg, *Legends*, 6:55, n. 284.

9. *HALOT*, 3:756.

10. *HALOT*, 4:1414.

11. Witton Davies, "Bel and the Dragon," in *Apocrypha*, vol. 1 of *The Apocrypha and Pseudepgripha of the Old Testament*, ed. R. H. Charles (Oxford: Clarendon, 1913), 658.

12. Sweeney, *Twelve Prophets,* 2:454. See, for example, Numbers 3:7–8; 8:26; 2 Chronicles 7:6; 8:14; 31:16–17; 35:2; Nehemiah 13:30.

13. James Bruckner, *Jonah, Nahum, Habakkuk, Zephaniah*, NIVAC (Grand Rapids, MI: Zondervan, 2004), 202.

14. Coggins and Han, *Six Minor Prophets*, 37.

15. For further elaboration of these views, see Theodore Heibert, "The Book of Habakkuk: Introduction, Commentary, and Reflections," in *Introduction to Apocalyptic Literature, Daniel, The Twelve Prophets*, NIB 7:626.

16. For an account of the manuscript evidence, see F. F. Bruce, "Habakkuk," in *Obadiah, Jonah, Micah, Nahum, and Habakkuk*, vol. 2 of *The Minor Prophets: An Exegetical and Expository Commentary*, ed. Thomas E. McComiskey (Grand Rapids, MI: Baker Academic, 1993), 836.

17. This event is also recorded in Jewish tradition; see Ginzberg, *Legends*, 4:348.

18. Hare, "Lives of the Prophets," 393.

19. For a description of these panels, including the one with Habakkuk, see Charles R. Morey, *Early Christian Art* (Princeton: Princeton University Press, 1953), 137–39. For illustrations, see Bill Storage, "The Door Panels of Santa Sabina," Rome101.com, September 1, 2016, http://rome101.com/Christian/Sabina/. For other artistic depictions of this scene throughout history, see Coggins and Han, *Six Minor Prophets*, 44–47.

20. See Coggins and Han, *Six Minor Prophets*, 42.

21. C. R. Morey, *Early Christian Art* (Princeton, NJ: Princeton University Press, 1953), 189–90; and Coggins and Han, *Six Minor Prophets*, 42.

22. Cited by Walther von Loewenich, *Martin Luther: The Man and His Work*, trans. Lawrence W. Denef (Minneapolis: Augsburg, 1982), 84; and Richard Marius, *Martin Luther: The Christian between God and Death* (Cambridge, MA: Belknap Press of Harvard University, 1999), 193.

23. "Calendar of Saints, Feasts, and Readings in the Orthodox Church," Greek Orthodox Archdiocese of America, www.goarch.org/chapel/calendar/.

24. See the Roman Martyrology provided online by the *Boston Catholic Journal* at www.boston-catholic-journal.com/roman-martrylogy-in-english/roman-martyrology-january-in-english.htm#January_15th.

ZEPHANIAH

1. Nevertheless, some scholars dispute this claim. See, for example, Mark W. Chavalas, "Zephaniah," *ZIBBC*, 5:182.

2. J. Alec Motyer, "Zephaniah," in *Zephaniah, Haggai, Zechariah, and Malachi*, vol. 3 of *The Minor Prophets: An Exegetical and Expository Commentary*, ed. Thomas E. McComiskey (Grand Rapids, MI: Baker Academic, 1998), 898.

3. Cited by John Lowden, *Illuminated Prophet Books: A Study of Byzantine Manuscripts of the Major and Minor Prophets* (University Park, PA: Pennsylvania State University Press, 1988), 52.

4. This is suggested, for example, by C. F. Pfeiffer, "Zephaniah," *The New Bible Dictionary* (Grand Rapids, MI: Eerdmans, 1962), 1358; and James Bruckner, *Jonah, Nahum, Habakkuk, Zephaniah*, NIVAC (Grand Rapids, MI: Zondervan, 2004), 277.

5. *HALOT*, 2:466.

6. Richard Coggins and Jin H. Han, *Six Minor Prophets through the Centuries* (Malden, MA: Wiley-Blackwell, 2011), 101–2.

7. John H. Walton, *Chronological and Background Charts of the Old Testament* (Grand Rapids, MI: Zondervan, 1994), 52.

8. Louis Ginzberg, *The Legends of the Jews*, 7 vols., trans. Henrietta Szold (Philadelphia: Jewish Publication Society, 1909–38), 6:386, n. 13.

9. O. S. Wintermute, *Apocalypse of Zephaniah: A New Translation and Introduction*, vol. 2 of *The Old Testament Pseudepigrapha*, ed. James H. Charlesworth (Garden City, NY: Doubleday, 1985), 499, 500–1 (for issues of dating). A translation of the surviving text of the *Apocalypse of Zephaniah* is provided on pp. 508–15.

10. Ginzberg, *Legends*, 5:130, n. 142.

11. "Calendar of Saints, Feasts, and Readings in the Orthodox Church," Greek Orthodox Archdiocese of America, www.goarch.org/chapel/calendar/.

12. See the Roman Martyrology provided online by the *Boston Catholic Journal* at www.boston-catholic-journal.com/roman-martrylogy-in-english/roman-martyrology-december-in-english.htm#December_3rd.

HAGGAI

1. The first king and founder of the Persian empire was Cyrus the Great. The second king was Cambyses, the son of Cyrus, who died under mysterious circumstances. See Kenneth G. Hoglund, "Haggai," *ZIBBC*, 5:194–95.

2. This opposition is recorded in Ezra 4–5.

3. For a discussion of the date of Zechariah's prophecies, see Kenneth L. Barker, "Zechariah," *EBC*, 8:726.

4. See Eugene H. Merrill, "Haggai," *EBC*, 8:702: "Haggai appears to identify himself with the old people who had seen the temple of Solomon in all of its glory some sixty-six years earlier (Hag 2:3; cf. Ezr 3:12). But there is no explicit testimony on his part that he had seen it with his own eyes."

5. Cited by John Lowden, *Illuminated Prophet Books: A Study of Byzantine Manuscripts of the Major and Minor Prophets* (University Park, PA: Pennsylvania State University Press, 1988), 52.

6. Richard Coggins and Jin H. Han, *Six Minor Prophets through the Centuries* (Malden, MA: Wiley-Blackwell, 2011), 140.

7. Coggins and Han, *Six Minor Prophets*, 135.

8. Louis Ginzberg, *The Legends of the Jews*, 7 vols., trans. Henrietta Szold (Philadelphia: Jewish Publication Society, 1909–38), 6:385–86, n. 13.

9. Ginzberg, *Legends*, 6:413, n. 76.

10. Its two short chapters contain just thirty-eight verses. The shortest book of the Old Testament, Obadiah, contains twenty-one verses.

11. This is according to Jesus himself. See John 5:39; Luke 24:25–27, 44.

12. Merrill, "Haggai," *EBC*, 8:701.

13. Raymond B. Dillard and Tremper Longman III, *An Introduction to the Old Testament*, rev. ed. (Grand Rapids, MI: Zondervan, 2006), 477.

14. This argument is made by Merrill, "Haggai," *EBC*, 8:701.

15. See also Coggins and Han, *Six Minor Prophets*, 136.

16. Dillard and Longman, *Introduction to the Old Testament*, 244.

17. Coggins and Han, *Six Minor Prophets*, 136.

18. "Calendar of Saints, Feasts, and Readings in the Orthodox Church," Greek Orthodox Archdiocese of America, www.goarch.org/chapel/calendar/.

19. See the Roman Martyrology provided online by the *Boston Catholic Journal* at www.boston-catholic-journal.com/roman-martrylogy-in-english/roman-martyrology-july-in-english.htm#July_4th.

ZECHARIAH

1. See previous chapter.

2. Richard Coggins and Jin H. Han, *Six Minor Prophets through the Centuries* (Malden, MA: Wiley-Blackwell, 2011), 153.

3. See Louis Ginzberg, *The Legends of the Jews*, 7 vols., trans. Henrietta Szold (Philadelphia: Jewish Publication Society, 1909–38), 4:354: "Among the band of returned exiles were the prophets Haggai, Zechariah, and Malachi"; and *Lives of the Prophets* 15:1: "Zechariah came from Chaldea when he was already well advanced in years."

4. See Raymond B. Dillard and Tremper Longman III, *An Introduction to the Old Testament*, rev. ed. (Grand Rapids, MI: Zondervan, 2006), 484: "If this identification is correct, Zechariah was a member of one of the families of priests who returned from the captivity; this would also serve to explain his familiarity with and interest in matters pertaining to the temple (e.g., 1:16; 3–4; 6:9–15; 8:9, 20–23; 14:16–21)."

5. Cited by John Lowden, *Illuminated Prophet Books: A Study of Byzantine Manuscripts of the Major and Minor Prophets* (University Park, PA: Pennsylvania State University Press, 1988), 51.

6. Kenneth L. Barker, "Zechariah," *EBC*, 8:747, suggests this as at least a possibility. Ben C. Ollenburger, "The Book of Zechariah," *NIB*, 7:758; and Thomas E. McComiskey, ed., "Zechariah," in *Zephaniah, Haggai, Zechariah, and Malachi*, vol. 3 of *The Minor Prophets: An Exegetical and Expository Commentary* (Grand Rapids, MI: Baker Academic, 1998), 898, present this as fact.

7. Coggins and Han, *Six Minor Prophets*, 135.

8. Ginzberg, *Legends*, 6:385–86, n. 13.

9. Dillard and Longman, *Introduction to the Old Testament*, 486.

10. Coggins and Han, *Six Minor Prophets*, 152.

11. See Angeline F. Schellenberg, "One in the Bond of War: The Unity of Deutero-Zechariah," *Didakalia* 12 (2001), 101; and James A. Hartle, "The Literary Unity of Zechariah," *JETS* 35 (1992), 145.

12. Coggins and Han, *Six Minor Prophets*, 151.

13. A fuller list of the evidence adduced to justify division of the book of Zechariah into two works instead of one is provided by Dillard and Longman, *Introduction to the Old Testament*, 487.

14. Dillard and Longman, *Introduction to the Old Testament*, 488.

15. McComiskey, "Zechariah," 3:1018.

16. Dillard and Longman, *Introduction to the Old Testament*, 489.

17. Coggins and Han, *Six Minor Prophets*, 151.

18. Coggins and Han, *Six Minor Prophets*, 150–51.

19. Coggins and Han, *Six Minor Prophets*, 151.

20. McComiskey, "Zechariah," 3:1003.

21. "Calendar of Saints, Feasts, and Readings in the Orthodox Church," Greek Orthodox Archdiocese of America, www.goarch.org/chapel/calendar/.

22. See the Roman Martyrology provided online by the *Boston Catholic Journal* at www.boston-catholic-journal.com/roman-martrylogy-in-english/roman-martyrology-september-in-english.htm#September_6th.

MALACHI

1. Louis Ginzberg, *The Legends of the Jews*, 7 vols., trans. Henrietta Szold (Philadelphia: Jewish Publication Society, 1909–38), 6:385–86, n. 13.

2. W. Neil, "Malachi," *IDB*, 3:229.

3. See, for example, Raymond B. Dillard and Tremper Longman III, *An Introduction to the Old Testament*, rev. ed. (Grand Rapids, MI: Zondervan, 2006), 498.

4. The author's translation of: .מַטָּל פְּתִגְמָא דַיוי עַל יִשְׂרָאֵל בְּיַד מַלְאֲכִי דִיתְקְרִי שְׁמֵיהּ עֶזְרָא סָפְרָא

5. Ginzberg, *Legends*, 4:354.

6. For the evidence to substantiate this dating, see Douglas Stuart, "Malachi," in *Zephaniah, Haggai, Zechariah, and Malachi*, vol. 3 of *The Minor Prophets: An Exegetical and Expository Commentary*, ed. Thomas E. McComiskey (Grand Rapids, MI: Baker Academic, 1998), 1252–53.

7. R. H. Pfeiffer, "Ezra," *IDB*, 2:214.

8. See Ginzberg, *Legends*, 6:432, n. 5.

9. W. Neil, "Malachi," *IDB*, 3:228.

10. See W. Neil, "Malachi," *IDB*, 228; and Eileen M. Schuller, "The Book of Malachi," *NIB*, 7:849.

11. W. Neil, "Malachi," *IDB*, 3:228–29.

12. Cited by John Lowden, *Illuminated Prophet Books: A Study of Byzantine Manuscripts of the Major and Minor Prophets* (University Park, PA: Pennsylvania State University Press, 1988), 51.

13. These parallels are explicated more fully by Douglas Stuart, "Malachi," 1394–95.

14. Stuart, "Malachi," 1395.

15. Ginzberg, *Legends*, 4:235.

16. Ginzberg, *Legends*, 6:385–86, n. 13.

17. W. Neil, "Malachi," *IDB*, 3:231.

18. "Calendar of Saints, Feasts, and Readings in the Orthodox Church," Greek Orthodox Archdiocese of America, www.goarch.org/chapel/calendar/.

19. See the Roman Martyrology provided online by the *Boston Catholic Journal* at www.boston-catholic-journal.com/roman-martrylogy-in-english/roman-martyrology-january-in-english.htm#January_14th.

INDEX OF NAMES

INDEX OF SCRIPTURE